eDiscovery
—Japan

eDiscovery —Japan

A PATHWAY FOR U.S. ATTORNEYS
TO DO BUSINESS WITH ASIAN CORPORATIONS

Masahiro Morimoto

GLOBAL TRY

Global Try is an imprint of UBIC, Inc.
www.ubicna.com
(650) 764-7664
bookinfo@ubicna.com

978-0-9914506-0-2 (paperback)
978-0-9914506-1-9 (ebook)

CONTENTS

———————O———————

Preface

·····················○·····················

How are companies with Asian roots and a global reach, such as Samsung, Toyota, Canon, Lenovo, and Foxconn, preparing to comply with the challenges of electronic legal discovery, or eDiscovery, as it is referred to today?

ASIAN COMPANIES' PREPAREDNESS FOR EDISCOVERY

In 2003, I started up an eDiscovery service provider in Japan called UBIC. Subsequently, the company began providing eDiscovery support services in the United States through three offices there. It also has support teams in Japan, South Korea, and Taiwan. In particular, UBIC has an outstanding track record as a provider of eDiscovery support services for Japanese companies. Thanks to its acclaimed technical prowess and support capability, UBIC went public in the U.S. on the NASDAQ Stock Market in 2013.

Since the founding of our company, we've expanded the scope of our business so that we can be a player in all fields of work related to discovery. We have also internally developed discovery review tools and software programs based on lawyers' needs. By applying the achievements of cutting-edge research in artificial intelligence, we've developed and commercialized predictive coding technology, which is machine-based, statistically driven software that makes it possible to reduce document review time drastically.

This book is written from the standpoint of a person who leads a successful eDiscovery service provider that serves Asian corporations. The book is intended mainly to give American lawyers an insight into Japanese companies' preparedness for, and approach to discovery. If you are a partner or an associate at a law firm that counts Japanese companies among its clients, you must correctly understand their circumstances. Lawyers intending to successfully act for Japanese client companies in discovery cases will find this book useful, as it explains the reality of eDiscovery in the Japanese business world. This book makes clear what lawyers should know about eDiscovery related to multi byte-character (Asian) languages, which is a challenge faced by eDiscovery providers in general. It also explains uniquely Japanese perspectives that may have implications for legal cases related to Japanese companies.

In addition, for lawyers wishing to improve relations with Japanese client companies, this book will provide clues on how to better communicate with them. There seems to be a great divide between Japanese businesspeople and

American lawyers. A certain divide is inevitable, of course, given the differences in their cultural backgrounds. What is important is for these two groups of professionals to understand their differences and respect each other so that their interactions may be harmonious and effective.

If you understand all these things—the legal, the technical, and the cultural—you will win the trust of Japanese companies and be able to develop long-lasting client-lawyer relationships with them so that you may serve as their essential partners in the field of litigation.

Masahiro Morimoto
January 2014

CHAPTER ONE

What's Occurring in the Field of Asian-Language eDiscovery?

T he growth of Asian companies is clear to see. Companies in Japan, my home country, as well as other Asian countries, including South Korea, Taiwan, and India, have remarkable growth potential. Countries like China and India are attractive markets partly because of their huge populations. Moreover, technological prowess has now become one of Asia's strengths.

Although there are ups and downs in the rankings of international competitiveness, we can still detect the promise of growth and innovation in Japanese companies, particularly in the information technology (IT) industry. While the Middle East and Africa also promise growth, Asian countries have the technological edge to spur innovation.

PROBLEMS ASSOCIATED WITH THE BUSINESS OF LITIGATION IN THE ASIAN MARKET

Naturally, Asian companies that have developed innovative products and services are trying to compete in the global arena. They are well aware that once they have advanced into Western markets they may risk involvement in various conflicts with local competitors. All the same, Japanese companies face a hidden challenge they rarely anticipate as they try to move into the Western markets: Dealing effectively with litigation—in particular, with eDiscovery procedures related to successful litigation—is this formidable new challenge.

Discovery itself is a significant procedure in that it enables the litigating parties to clarify the points of dispute before entering trial proceedings, by disclosing evidence to each other in advance. To my mind, this procedure embodies the fairness of the American legal system. eDiscovery, which is the forensically sound collection, processing, search, review, and production of electronically sourced information (ESI), is a major segment of the legal discovery process and is increasingly relevant in every area of business operation.

Unfortunately, Japanese companies have several disadvantages in discovery. One of the greatest of these concerns is the cost of discovery work. Japanese companies operating in Western markets are said to pay a litigation cost per case that is more than double what is paid by American companies on average. The bulk of the litigation cost paid by Japanese companies is related to discovery work, including translation of Japanese documents into English.

In addition, there is a scarcity of eDiscovery service providers that are capable of accurately identifying and extracting documents containing evidence by analyzing a database of files written in Japanese, which, unlike English, is a multibyte-character language.

If an inept eDiscovery provider is employed, the cost of discovery is likely to spiral up from the initial estimate because of unforeseen problems. Processing costs specific to the Japanese language pose a problem that companies in English-speaking countries do not have to worry about.

JAPANESE COMPANIES HAVE SPECIFIC DISADVANTAGES IN EDISCOVERY

Regarding eDiscovery, Japanese companies are at a disadvantage compared with American and European companies in the four following respects. Lawyers who count Japanese companies among their clients should be prepared to overcome these obstacles.

Electronic Data Are Not Recorded in English

First of all, there is the problem of extra costs that Japanese companies have to pay because of their use of the Japanese language, as I already mentioned. Most Japanese corporate documents are written and stored in Japanese. As a result, if a Japanese company outsources eDiscovery work to a U.S. service provider, the cost estimate presented by the provider is certain to be higher than in the case of comparable eDiscovery work for an American company.

In addition, the possibility is slim that the actual cost will be in line with the estimate. In many cases, a significant cost overrun arises because of problems specific to the Japanese language, such as the frequent occurrence of character garbling, inaccurate searches, and data errors.

Moreover, documents and email messages must be translated into English. Proposing solutions that minimize the translation cost will be appreciated by your Japanese client companies, as translation costs often spiral up.

Lack of Information about eDiscovery

A second issue is that Japanese companies are not well-informed about eDiscovery. While eDiscovery is a procedure commonly used under the U.S. legal system, it is not as well-known in Asian countries such as Japan and South Korea, although requests for disclosure of documents are occasionally made as a legal procedure in those countries. In short, most Japanese companies have never experienced eDiscovery work. They are unfamiliar with the process of extracting materials containing evidence from their computers, memory devices, and paper documents. As a result, when they select an eDiscovery provider in U.S. litigations, they often will turn to U.S. lawyers for advice.

If you can convince a Japanese client company of your ability to choose an eDiscovery provider best suited to the case, the client will feel comfortable with putting you in charge of the case. Of course, using discovery support tools or systems developed by native speakers of the Japanese language and recommending a Japanese eDiscovery provider also will be welcomed by your Japanese clients.

Absence of Guidelines Concerning eDiscovery

Japan has not established any legislation or regulations concerning eDiscovery. While a number of Japanese companies are entangled in U.S. litigations each year and pay litigation costs in the billions of dollars, there are not any official guidelines for dealing with eDiscovery. A third major issue to confront is that Japanese companies face various risks when they transfer data to the United States for discovery work by U.S. providers.

For example, a U.S. federal appeals court ruled in 2010 that subpoenas seeking nonprivileged material of foreign origin could be enforced against the law firms in possession of documents belonging to overseas clients in aid of a grand jury investigation into those clients (In re Grand Jury Subpoenas, No. 10-15758, slip op. at19638 [9th Cir. Dec. 7, 2010]). The ruling suggests the possibility that disclosure orders by U.S. government agencies such as the FBI as well as U.S. courts may be enforced against electronic data held by companies in Japan that are not supposed to be under U.S. jurisdiction.

Disclosure could pose a threat to the protection not only of corporate information held by Japanese companies, but to Japanese national security information as well. However, Japan has not established any legislation or regulation that deals with such risk. Consequently, for now, Japanese companies must exercise their own discretion in protecting their intellectual property. If you understand this situation and propose the best possible solutions for Japanese companies, you will be able to win their trust.

Japanese companies are at a disadvantage regarding the use of eDiscovery in several respects, as described above. However, seen from a different angle, these disadvantages could lead to plenty of opportunities for U.S. lawyers to win Japanese companies as clients. If you understand the difficulties facing Japanese companies in the field of eDiscovery and proactively propose solutions to overcome these particular difficulties, you may set yourself apart from your competitors. The eDiscovery support business targeting Japanese companies is growing. Japanese companies themselves are well aware of the increasing importance of securing eDiscovery support.

When I started UBIC as an eDiscovery service provider specializing in Asian languages, there was little awareness of the importance of eDiscovery services among Japanese companies. Whenever I talked about eDiscovery at seminars, I was greeted with skeptical questions like "Why should we prepare for eDiscovery?" and "Do we really have to prepare for eDiscovery?" Now, however, I am seldom given the cold shoulder or meet with skepticism when I talk to Japanese corporate legal officers about eDiscovery. This is an indication of how far Japanese companies have come in understanding the need to prepare for eDiscovery. It also suggests that business opportunities are proliferating for lawyers willing to incorporate eDiscovery into their litigation strategy.

It is also true that corporate legal officers at Japanese companies are less prone than before to blindly follow the instructions of lawyers. As an indication of the growing interest in eDiscovery in Japan, we receive increasingly in-depth questions from corporate legal officers about the specifics of eDiscovery work and how to prepare for eDiscovery. This is not a phenomenon limited to major companies. Smaller companies have come to recognize the need to prepare for eDiscovery in case they are involved in U.S. litigations. eDiscovery is attracting increasing attention and has become a popular topic at corporate legal offices in Japan.

Japanese companies tend to prefer developing long-term relationships with lawyers in whom they have placed trust. Now is the time to act if you want to win Japanese companies as clients in eDiscovery cases and cultivate long-term relationships with them before the Japanese market for eDiscovery matures.

Lack of Willingness to Develop eDiscovery Solutions Tailored to Japanese Companies

A number of American lawyers and service providers are eager to win Japanese companies as clients in eDiscovery cases. At the same time, however, they have worries about and see risks in the Japanese market. Their worries stem from their perception that eDiscovery cases involving Japanese companies are problematic. Even experienced lawyers regard Japan as a difficult eDiscovery market.

eDiscovery cases involving Japanese-language documents are certainly difficult to handle. Japanese-language documents cannot be analyzed with the same eDiscovery tools as those used in the analysis of English-language documents. Providers may be annoyed by the frequent occurrence of character garbling and the need to cope with unfamiliar software applications. I also have the sense that as of yet there is little willingness in the U.S. litigation industry to discuss eDiscovery-related problems arising in Japan. Probably, nobody dares to initiate such discussions because there is no standard for providing fundamental solutions.

Some U.S. lawyers and providers already working for Japanese companies in eDiscovery cases have apparently been muddling through without a proper understanding of uniquely Japanese problems. U.S. discovery providers' handling of Japanese-language documents is in such a sorry state that many questionable practices are ongoing, and this may be another reason for the lack of discussions about Japanese-language eDiscovery. If an industrywide working group is created to discuss Japanese-language eDiscovery, for example, substantive discussions would be impossible because such practices cannot be mentioned. These practices include:

- Submitting documents containing garbled characters without making corrections.
- Translating unnecessary documents without understanding their relevance.
- Submitting documents without checking whether translations are accurate.

The above are a few examples of questionable practices that service providers cannot afford to discuss in public. I assume that the presence of such practices may be stifling constructive discussions about knowledge, techniques, and procedures that may solve eDiscovery problems related to Japanese and other Asian languages.

SIX COMMON MISCONCEPTIONS ABOUT JAPANESE COMPANIES

In this section, I will address certain prevailing misconceptions about Japanese companies, which are not uncommon among American lawyers. To my understanding, there are roughly six major misconceptions, which are as follows.

- "Japanese companies naturally understand discovery."

- "Garbling of Japanese texts is unavoidable."
- "Japanese-language documents must be translated before going through the eDiscovery process."
- "It is unavoidable that Japanese-language documents cost more to process and take longer to review than English documents."
- "Japanese companies are unwilling to follow lawyers' instructions."
- "Japanese companies are institutionally secretive."

All of the preceding statements are misconceptions. Below, I will discuss each in more detail.

Misconception 1.
"Japanese companies naturally understand discovery."

First, let us look at the level of Japanese companies' awareness about eDiscovery. In the United States, many ordinary people as well as litigation professionals are aware of discovery as a legal procedure. What you must understand is that in Japan there is a near-total lack of awareness of legal discovery (when Japanese people hear of the word *discovery*, what comes to their mind are things like the Space Shuttle Discovery and the Discovery TV channel). Awareness of legal discovery is gradually growing in Japan, particularly among major companies. Still, most people are unaware of or have an inaccurate understanding of discovery.

I assume that when instructed by lawyers to prepare and submit documents, corporate legal officers in Japan follow the instructions without knowing whether they are part of discovery or other litigation procedures. However, it does not mean that they are content with doing lawyers' bidding. They must be feeling a sense of uneasiness and uncertainty. Submitting classified corporate information, including that on intellectual property, such as patents and trademarks, without understanding the reason or purpose would be an extremely stressful experience for anyone.

Discovery involving Japanese companies rarely goes smoothly. In many cases, Japanese companies face long schedule delays and are charged huge extra fees in the millions of dollars. Secretly, many Japanese companies may feel an urge to protest to lawyers and ask them hard questions. In reality, however, they refrain from expressing themselves openly because of the unique Japanese sense of virtue, which forbids self-assertion as a disrespectful behavior. The resultant lack of communication is one reason why Japanese companies make little progress in understanding discovery.

That is also why corporate legal officers at Japanese companies are likely to appreciate it when American lawyers conscientiously educate them about discovery, a U.S. legal procedure unfamiliar to them, thereby dispelling their sense of uncertainty. Such conscientious service will surely be valued by Japanese companies.

"How does the discovery procedure work?"

"Why is it necessary?"

"What should Japanese companies do?"

"What work do eDiscovery providers do?"

"How much does it cost?"

"What is the security status of a huge amount of data that must be sent to (and stored at) a review server?"

"Where is the data center?"

"Who will translate documents that will eventually be submitted as evidence?"

You may think it is not necessary to talk to clients about discovery-related issues like these unless consulted by them first. However, if you initiate your clients into the unfamiliar world of discovery before they ask such questions, you will win their hearts.

I know of a handful of American lawyers who carefully look after Japanese client companies unfamiliar with discovery. All of them have won their clients' trust and are expanding their business and winning new clients in Japan. These trusted attorneys spend just an hour or so on briefing their Japanese clients on the discovery procedure with a few pages of presentation materials before going into a case, and they are rewarded with words of appreciation such as, "We have never received such conscientious service from lawyers" and "We would like to put you in charge of all of our cases."

One corporate legal officer that I know of assesses the quality of lawyers based on how they answer questions concerning eDiscovery.

We Japanese are a people who feel a strong sense of obligation to return favors to people who carefully look after us, and our actions may be influenced by that sense. Careful attention to clients' needs could clinch a deal for you in a multimillion-dollar case.

Misconception 2.
"Garbling of Japanese texts is unavoidable."

There seems to be a consensus among discovery providers that eDiscovery in cases involving Japanese companies is problematic. That view is not wrong. Compared with English, so-called multibyte-character languages, which include Chinese, Japanese, and Korean, necessitate a high level of analytical techniques.

While the problem of garbling affects the whole of eDiscovery work, the presence of garbled characters is recognized during the review process in particular. In principle, during the preliminary review, Japanese-language-capable eDiscovery service providers review and classify Japanese files before translation. This arrangement reduces the translation cost by eliminating unnecessary translation work.

However, some providers demand that all files be translated before the preliminary review. That would push up the translation cost unnecessarily, so a demand like that should be rejected.

The problem is that many lawyers believe that garbling of Japanese texts is unavoidable. This is obviously a misconception that must be corrected.

As I will explain in Chapter 2, it is possible to avoid character garbling. I can say that with certainty because the analytical tools developed by my company can almost entirely eliminate garbling. If you employ providers equipped with advanced techniques, you can avoid the garbling of Japanese texts.

If providers insist that garbling of Japanese texts is unavoidable, it would be an indication to me of their lack of capability to handle Japanese-language discovery. Even though they may provide high-quality, English-language eDiscovery services, it would be wise to turn to other providers in eDiscovery cases related to Japanese companies.

Misconception 3.
"Japanese-language documents must be translated before going through the eDiscovery process."

Some providers demand that all Japanese-language files, including documents and emails, be translated into English before being analyzed. A demand like that is a convenient excuse for the providers' lack of adequate tools. Selecting a provider equipped with Japanese-language-capable analytical tools makes prediscovery translation an unnecessary process. Actually, prediscovery translation is nothing more than wasteful work. Moreover, it could expose clients to various risks.

There are three risks. The first is that the meaning of texts may be altered through translation. Even skilled translators cannot always translate Japanese into English completely faithfully. If proper nouns, including the names of people, places, and products are mistyped, keyword-based searches may fail to identify relevant documents. In other words, the quality of translation could have significant implications for the quality of discovery work.

Japanese people quite often use the phrase *"Yoroshiku onegai shimasu,"* for example. The problem is that the meaning of the phrase varies significantly depending on the context or circumstances. The phrase may mean any of the following:

- "I thank you for your kindness/hard work in advance."
- "I beg your kindness for my children."
- "Send my regards to XX."

This phrase may cause confusion in the investigation of antitrust cases, for example, because it is difficult to determine in which sense the phrase was used. Translations that fail to take into account Japanese culture and society may increase the risk that evidentiary materials that should not go to the opposing party could be submitted erroneously. In particular, when translation is done before the discovery process, the risk is higher that files containing inaccurate translations of ambiguous phrases and words will be submitted as evidence. In principle, document analysis related to eDiscovery should be conducted before translation of the original documents.

The second risk is cost. In preparation for eDiscovery, a database of information is created in order to extract documents containing evidence for disclosure out of tens of thousands of pages of data. If the discovery work is outsourced to a provider incapable of analyzing Japanese-language documents, translation should be done before evidentiary materials are identified. In that case, the volume of data to be translated could be several times the volume of data that is actually necessary as evidence.

Needless to say, companies operating in Japan, except for some foreign-affiliated ones, prepare and store documents in Japanese. (Although some companies have recently adopted English as an official company language, most of their past documents are presumed to have been written and stored in Japanese.) As I mentioned earlier, providers with insufficient technical expertise have difficulty appropriately conducting Japanese-language keyword searches, and as a result, it may become necessary to translate into English all potentially responsive documents. The translation cost alone could amount to millions of dollars. Moreover, it could turn out that only 10 percent of the translated documents are actually used in discovery. Most of the translation would be wasted effort.

In principle, only documents to be submitted to the opposing party should be translated. Performing translation before extracting the necessary documents is an inefficient approach. The costs associated with this approach could potentially become a heavy burden on your Japanese client companies. In one case I know of, the translation cost alone amounted to more than 3 billion yen (roughly $29 million dollars) because translation was done before the extraction process.

In many cases, the cost could be reduced by millions of dollars if a Japanese-language capable discovery provider is employed from the beginning so as to extract necessary data alone.

The third risk is information leakage. This is the risk that client Japanese companies may unwittingly pass classified, confidential, or sensitive corporate information to the outside. Information leakage could not only affect individual cases, it could pose a threat to the entire company.

The following rumor, which had circulated widely in the litigation industry, may give you an idea of the seriousness of the risk of information leakage that may arise during discovery.

A Japanese company employed a foreign provider as a discovery support service provider. Personal computers sent to the United States for investigation contained data on planned bid prices in bidding for energy business contracts. On the Japanese side, price information was under strict control, with only a handful of persons allowed access to the price data. But a major U.S. company somehow obtained the price information.

Potentially responsive information may include classified corporate information, such as patents, business strategies, market research data, and email exchanges among top executives. Translation of a vast amount of classified information may be outsourced to contractors and subcontractors. The security of classified information subject to translation is paramount. All possible measures to ensure the security of the information should be taken.

This risk is particular to Japanese companies that need to translate documents as part of the discovery process. American companies do not face an information leakage risk of this kind. Should an information leakage occur during the discovery process, the lawyer handling the case may be held accountable.

Misconception 4.
"It is unavoidable that Japanese-language documents cost more and take longer to review than English documents."

Many American lawyers believe that Japanese-language discovery is problematic. This belief leads to the assumption that it is unavoidable that discovery work related to Japanese companies takes more time and costs more than work related to American companies. That assumption is wrong.

In many cases, discovery work related to Japanese companies may be more time-consuming and costly, but only because the provider is using discovery tools, including processing and review tools, that are not Japanese-language-capable. Problems like these disrupt the discovery work, making it necessary to repeat previous processes or to implement processes that would otherwise be unnecessary (for example, translation and conversion to TIFF or OCR), resulting in a cost overrun. As I mentioned earlier, such problems can be avoided by employing a Japanese-language-capable discovery provider.

Some discovery providers are increasing the efficiency of eDiscovery by applying predictive coding, which is becoming the mainstream technique in the eDiscovery field, for the analysis of Japanese-language documents. As a result, the difference in time and cost between Japanese-language and English-language discovery work is presumed to have been largely eliminated. If you believe it is inevitable that Japanese-language documents cost more and take longer to review than English documents, you should discard that idea as an obsolete prejudice.

Misconception 5.
"Japanese companies are unwilling to follow lawyers' instructions."

The fifth misconception concerns American lawyers' perception of Japanese companies. Several U.S. lawyers who are acquaintances of mine have told me they share the presumption that Japanese companies are unwilling to follow the instructions of lawyers. When I asked them for explanations, one said that Japanese companies find faults with his instructions, while another cited Japanese companies' insistence on making decisions only after all details have been checked.

Most lawyers believe that Japanese companies' apparent reluctance to follow lawyers' instructions is attributable to the intrinsic culture of Japanese companies (and so they assume it cannot be helped). However, this behavior has nothing to do with the intrinsic culture of the companies. The real reason that Japanese companies cannot make these decisions is that they are poorly informed about legal procedures such as discovery.

As I explained at the beginning, Japanese companies suffer from a significant lack of information and knowledge about discovery. Corporate legal officers at Japanese companies are at a loss as to how to explain lawyers' instructions to other people within the company and whether or not it is possible that they will somehow be held personally accountable. They want lawyers to dispel their uncertainty over such questions. They are being cautious because of their uncertainty. If you understand this and take care to help corporate legal officers in their internal communications efforts, they will feel reassured.

Misconception 6.
"Japanese companies are institutionally secretive."

The sixth and final misconception that should be shed is that Japanese companies are institutionally secretive. I've heard Americans complain: "During meetings, Japanese workers whisper among themselves with an air of conspiracy" and "Japanese workers answer questions with just a smile accompanied by a vague tilt of the head, instead of saying yes or no."

The scenes described by complaints like these are nothing unusual in the Japanese workplace. However, it is not that Japanese workers are trying to conceal secrets or using deceptive tactics. People who will provide eDiscovery services to Japanese companies for the first time should become familiar with the characteristics of Japanese companies explained in Chapter 4 and try to find out what these companies may really think or want.

If you shed all six commonly held misconceptions about Japanese companies, your perception of these companies will likely change significantly. If you are still stuck with these misconceptions, you may need to learn more about:

- Providers of eDiscovery catering to Japanese companies.
- Concepts and thought processes unique to Japanese companies.

If you are to become a lawyer of choice for Japanese companies, you must definitely learn more about these two topics.

TWO KEY REQUIREMENTS FOR BECOMING A LAWYER OF CHOICE FOR JAPANESE COMPANIES

As an American, two key requirements for becoming a lawyer of choice for Japanese companies are being able to:

- Determine the discovery service provider's Japanese-language capability so you may take care to prevent your Japanese clients from suffering undue stress during the eDiscovery process.
- Understand how most Japanese companies think, so you may communicate with your clients skillfully through means that they appreciate and find easy to understand.

If you meet the two key requirements, you will be able not only to smoothly implement litigation procedures, including discovery, on behalf of Japanese client companies, but also give them better satisfaction. The knack is to convince Japanese companies that you understand their needs and make them feel comfortable with putting you in charge of their cases. Stress your ability to meet the two key requirements, and you will obtain the trust of Japanese companies and win them as new clients.

Unlike previously, some Japanese companies are aware of their lack of information and knowledge concerning discovery, as well as a shortage of sufficient discovery support. As Japanese companies are loath to be kept in the dark, you can put them at ease by helping them become better informed. They are waiting for someone to propose discovery solutions so that they can avoid various discovery-related risks and reduce costs. Because there is a scarcity of lawyers who can propose fundamental solutions to Japanese companies and help them deal with litigation more effectively, if you can meet the two key requirements we've identified, you will be able to become a lawyer of choice for Japanese companies engaged in U.S. litigation.

Before discussing the two key requirements in detail, let us take a look at what is occurring in the field of Japanese-language eDiscovery in the next chapter.

CHAPTER TWO

Japanese-Language Issues in eDiscovery

───────────○───────────

W hat is occurring in the field of Japanese-language eDiscovery? What issues lead to the perception that Japanese-language eDiscovery is problematic?

In this chapter, I will explain the current situation of Japanese-language eDiscovery from the viewpoint that it is problem prone. Unless you understand the fundamental factors that underlie problems related to Japanese-language eDiscovery, you cannot deliver fundamental solutions— even though you may be able to provide stopgap measures.

I presume that most lawyers who have handled cases involving Japanese companies have encountered uniquely Japanese issues in the legal setting and have been challenged by the difficulty these issues often create in such cases. For example, it is said that most Japanese client companies typically respond to their lawyers' instructions in either of two ways: no reaction or an extreme reaction.

Issues of eDiscovery that would be unlikely or even unimaginable in cases related to U.S. companies crop up one after another without the knowledge of lawyers. As a result, lawyers may be surprised at the sudden arrival of alarming messages like, "The review will be extended for a week, as massive character garbling has been found" and "We can't prepare documents in time for tomorrow's deposition because we need more time for the processing of Japanese-language documents."

Uniquely Japanese eDiscovery problems can be classified into two categories. Problems in the first category are those that are attributable to institutional factors such as slow decision making. Problems in the second category are the result of technical glitches related to the eDiscovery process.

First-category problems can be avoided to some degree by improving communications with Japanese client companies and by better understanding their corporate culture. In other words, lawyers can avoid such problems through their own efforts (I will discuss this point in more detail in Chapter 4).

Second-category problems resulting from technical glitches can be avoided by using eDiscovery tools developed by a Japanese discovery provider and employing a Japanese discovery support provider as a support service provider. Therefore, I will explain the viewpoints from which to select eDiscovery providers suited to your Japanese client companies.

CAUSES OF COMMON PROBLEMS IN JAPANESE-LANGUAGE EDISCOVERY

Many of the discovery providers I know of explain that eDiscovery involving Japanese companies is problematic and therefore burdensome. For example, it is necessary to deal with character garbling and analyze messages sent via email software programs used only in Japan or developed internally by Japanese companies. This is an irritating problem for all service providers.

In principle, there should be nothing difficult about eDiscovery, which is merely a procedure for collecting and disclosing evidence. However, this proves to be a difficult process in cases related to Japanese companies. To put it more precisely, in eDiscovery cases related to Japanese companies, resourceful solutions are needed to address problems unique to Japanese companies.

There are three typical causes of problems that arise in Japanese-language discovery.

- The Japanese-language uses unique character codes
- It is difficult to distinguish separate words in Japanese text

• A wide variety of customized software applications are used in Japan

Let us examine these causes in detail one by one.

Cause 1.
The Japanese Language Uses Unique Character Codes

Asian languages, known as multibyte-character languages (meaning, languages using multibyte character sets), cannot be appropriately processed unless they are processed in different ways from English. A *multibyte character set* is a term that refers to a set of characters represented by two or more bytes of data. Usually when people are speaking of multibyte-character languages, they are referring to Chinese, Japanese, and Korean. A one-byte character set is a set of characters represented by one byte of data (see Figure 2.1).

The Character Codes Are Unique

Character Code	A	B	C	Data Per Character
ASCII	41	42	43	1 byte
Kanji Characters				
Unicode	E6,BC,A2		E5,A5,97	3 bytes
Shift JIS	8A,BF		8E,9A	2 bytes
JIS	34,41		38,A	2 bytes
EUC	B4,C1		BB,FA	2 bytes

Figure 2.1. Texts written in those Asian languages known as "two-byte character languages" cannot be appropriately processed unless they are treated differently from English.

In the world of computers, one byte of data can represent 256 different values. One byte is sufficient to represent the character set of the English alphabet, for example. However, it is not sufficient to represent all of the characters that exist in the Chinese language. Therefore, two bytes of data, which can represent up to 65,536 (256 to the power of two) different values are used to represent a set of Chinese characters that are in practical use.

Because of the coding difference, eDiscovery providers who are not capable of handling multibyte-character languages cannot appropriately perform Japanese-language eDiscovery work. For example, such providers cannot appropriately conduct Japanese language, keyword-based searches or accurately display Japanese texts on the screen of a review tool. In some cases, technically challenged providers try to skip over these problems by proposing to convert all data to petrified formats like PDF and TIFF and process them through optical character recognition (OCR).

Cause 2.
It Is Difficult to Distinguish Separate Words in Japanese Text

Using a space to separate words makes it easy to distinguish them. When reading English, readers can easily recognize individual words because of the presence of a space between separate words. By contrast, Asian languages do not use spaces in the same way as English.

In Japanese, spaces are not used to separate words. The presence of various types of characters, including the *hiragana* and *katakana* syllabaries, and Chinese characters, helps in the recognition of individual words in Japanese sentences. A syllabary is a set of written characters representing syllables (in some languages or stages of writing) serving the purpose of an alphabet. Although *kutouten*, which correspond to punctuation marks in English, are used to make it easier to identify the sentence structure, Japanese-language documents require a much higher level of analytical technique. English certainly requires some analytical knowledge, such as unifying verb inflections, and yet processing English texts is not as complicated as processing

Japanese texts, for instance because it is difficult to separate words (see Figure 2.2).

It Is Difficult to Distinguish Separate Words

今日は対象の半導体デバイス構造の特許訴訟に関して弁護士と meetingしました。

今日 | は | 対象 | の | 半導体 | デバイス | 構造 | の | 特許 | 訴訟 | に | 関して | 弁護士 | と | meeting | しま | した。

Figure 2.2. In English texts, the presence of a space between separate words makes it easy to distinguish them. In Japanese, spaces are not used as a way to distinguish separate words. Translation of above line: "Today, we had a meeting with a lawyer regarding the patent case for targeted semiconductor device structure."

Cause 3.
A Wide Variety of Customized Software Applications Are Used in Japan

Unlike U.S. companies, where the concept of open innovation has long been entrenched, Japanese companies are basically internally oriented. Although they have now come to use common formats and software programs to some degree, most Japanese companies believed until around 2000 that internally developing business systems and software programs was the key to strengthening their competitiveness. Consequently, the offices of Japanese companies are cluttered with internally developed software applications. It is not unusual for a Japanese company to internally develop a mail server or a PDF-producing program, for example.

Although passion for self-sufficiency in technology may be a wellspring of Japan's technological prowess, the use of internally developed applications could cause problems in the discovery process because it is difficult to customize discovery tools to work with the unique applications.

Japanese-language eDiscovery is problematic as a result of the three major causes we've already discussed in this chapter. Next, we will take a look at specific problems.

EDISCOVERY PROBLEMS INVOLVING DATA HELD BY JAPANESE COMPANIES

I would say that few lawyers, including experienced ones, accurately understand what is occurring in the field of eDiscovery involving data held by Japanese companies. Basically, lawyers see eDiscovery evidence after relevant data have been handled by eDiscovery service providers. Based on our vast experience as an eDiscovery provider supporting Japanese companies, we have developed eDiscovery processes tailored to processing Japanese-language (Asian-language) documents and use them systematically.

As shown in the table below, we prevent character garbling during the review process and eliminate work duplications by carefully consulting with clients about issues specific to the Japanese language in each process. However, many other providers try a one-size-fits-all approach, applying the same method and tools regardless of whether the data being handled are written in Japanese or English.

EDRM Stages	UBIC Stages
Preservation	Special Consulting for Asian Environment (Collection)
Collection	Collection/Paper Scan
Processing	Special Consulting for Asian Environment (Processing)
	Asian Application Process
	Processing
Analysis	Special Consulting for Asian Environment (Analysis)
	Analysis
Review	Review Professional Services (In other Asian languages)
	Review
	Translation
Production	Production

■ Special Services Asian Language

▨ Consulting

▨ Service

▭ Other

■ EDRM Phase

What should be kept in mind is that evidence you see has been extracted as a result of various solutions (dubious quick fixes in some cases) performed by the eDiscovery services provider.

It is essential for you to be aware of what problems have arisen and how they have been solved during discovery. That is not only because you must prepare yourself to provide explanations when requested by your Japanese client companies, but because you need to draw up roadmaps and strategies for tackling future problems.

Problems in the Review Process

Garbling. The most frequent problem related to eDiscovery involving data held by Japanese companies is character garbling. Garbling is so much associated with Japanese-language eDiscovery in particular that the Japanese word for "garbling," *mojibake*, is used among some non-Japanese-speaking eDiscovery experts (see Figure 2.3).

Character Garbling

```
 1    ,¨¢ϑ        -¼ŽŒ-ƒT•ÏÚ'±        ,¨¢ϑ
 2    ,É    •ŽŒ-Ši•ŽŒ-ˆê"Ê     ,É
 3    ,É,è      "®ŽŒ-Ž©§          ,É,è
 4    ,Ü,·    •"®ŽŒ     ,Ü,·
 5    B    <L†-<å"       B
 6    æ¶    -¼ŽŒ- ˆê"Ê     æ¶
 7    ‰‰½    -¼ŽŒ-"    ‰‰½
 8    "x    -¼ŽŒ-Ú"ö-•"ŽŒ        "x
 9    ,à    •ŽŒ-ŒW•ŽŒ     ,à
10    ,·,Y      "®ŽŒ-Ž©—§         ,·,þ
11    ,Ü,¹    •"® ŽŒ    ,Ü,·
12    ,ñ    •"®ŽŒ      ,ñ
13    B    <L†-<å"       B
14    æ,Ù,Ç    -¼ŽŒ- ˆê"Ê       æ,Ù,Ç
15    ,Ì    •ŽŒ-A'Ì‰»     ,Ì
16    —    -¼ŽŒ- ˆê"Ê    —
17    ,½,¢      -¼ŽŒ- ˆê"Ê    ,½,¢
```

Figure 2.3. Garbling characters is among the most common problems in eDiscovery work involving data held by Japanese companies.

The important thing to remember is that the presence of character garbling is not recognized until processed texts are displayed on the screen during the review process.

In the eDiscovery process, collected and processed documents are uploaded to a review tool. During document processing, many service providers cannot judge whether or not the data files being processed contain garbled characters. They recognize garbled characters, if any, for the first time when they open the files at the time of review. When garbled characters are found, the providers have to look for and identify the raw, unprocessed data and upload them again after resolving garbling. As a result, the review time and cost increase significantly.

When our company handles an eDiscovery case, we require each reviewer to perform the review process at an average speed of 80 files per hour if only a simple classification is needed. The minimum hourly wage for reviewers is $70 dollars. The cost increases each time the review work is suspended because of garbling. The hosting cost also grows as a result of the need for uploading data more than once.

If you believe that character garbling is nothing more than a minor problem in your discovery project, you should think again. Although correcting garbled data may appear to be simple work, the extra time and cost required will be damaging to your clients.

If the problem of garbling became non-existent, how would eDiscovery work for your Japanese client companies change? The necessary time and cost could be reduced drastically.

Optimizing the cost. If the problem of garbling is eliminated, the cost of processing and reviewing data can be optimized. There will be no need to pay fees to providers for the extra work to resolve garbling, including correcting garbled data and repeating processes. That could drastically reduce the cost of eDiscovery. And, as clients do not have to worry about extra expenses that might otherwise be charged, a benefit of this outcome is that clients may feel at this point that they can afford to allocate a more generous budget for legal services.

Speeding up work. The absence of garbling would significantly speed up the discovery process by eliminating the extra time necessary for solving the garbling problem, thereby reducing the risk of schedule delays. Speedier work makes it possible to identify evidence at an earlier date, providing more time for mapping out litigation strategy.

The important fact for American lawyers to recognize is that the problem of garbling can be avoided. Many service providers may assert that garbling is an unavoidable problem. However, that is not correct. They make such an assertion because they are incapable of preventing garbling due to technical inferiority. You may rest assured that the problem of garbling can be avoided by competent service providers.

If lawyers allow this problem to continue, on the grounds that it cannot be solved even by a major provider, and at a huge cost, they would be doing a disservice to their clients. If appropriate procedures are followed, garbling can be avoided.

The important thing for lawyers to do is to propose solutions for the issue before being consulted by clients.

Problems in Production

Next, we will look at problems related to production, which may involve unrealized, potentially huge risks. Specifically, such problems include the failure to produce evidence that should have been produced and the submission of documents that should not have been submitted (adverse evidence).

If evidence is mishandled because of the lack of capability of the eDiscovery provider at the time of production of depositions, when the treatment of the attorney-client privilege is critically important, the case would immediately take a turn for the worse for your client. However, problems like this rarely come to public attention. In many cases, major service providers manage to sweep problems under the rug through some quick fix or other. If such problems come to light, the lawyers involved could be held accountable as well.

It is doubtful whether all providers are systematically prepared to prevent problems related to production. It would be too late to regret having employed an inferior provider after a problem has already occurred.

The Dubious Claim to Be
Japanese-Language Capable

Another problem sometimes encountered is that eDiscovery providers claiming to be Japanese-language capable are not necessarily capable of performing the full range of eDiscovery processes. In their sales pitches, service providers may offer reassuring explanations that they can handle multibyte character languages and have no difficulty handling Japanese-language documents. You should counter such sweet-talk by asking specific questions like, "Are your analytical and review tools Japanese-language capable?"

Claims of *multilanguage capability* and *multibyte capability* are ubiquitous in promotional brochures for eDiscovery tools, but many such tools prove to be ineffective in Japanese-language eDiscovery.

Tools claiming to be multilanguage capable may indeed be sufficient to perform the simple task of data collection in many cases. However, in the more sophisticated process of analysis, most of the so-called multilanguage tools reveal their inability to handle Japanese-language documents. As I mentioned earlier, the three typical causes are that:

- The Japanese language uses unique character codes.
- It is difficult to distinguish separate words.
- A wide variety of unique software applications are used in Japan.

If you employ an eDiscovery provider that uses inadequate tools, the results could be disastrous. The processes of analyzing and sorting collected data would be bogged down, and the review would go on and on amid piles of garbled data, swelling discovery fees. If the review process fails to go smoothly, it could become impossible to meet the deadline for the production of evidence, putting your clients at a disadvantage in litigation.

Presence or Absence of Forensic Skills

Finally, let us take a look at problems that may arise from eDiscovery service providers' lack of digital forensic skills. eDiscovery work, which seeks to identify and extract documents, email messages, and other texts containing evidence from among a vast amount of data, is like scouring a desert looking for a lost diamond ring.

Sometimes, evidence extracted in the eDiscovery process may be judged to be not valid as evidence because of some technical defect or other minute, but significant alteration in the data. If a recovered diamond ring was broken, skillful repair work would be necessary. Likewise, if identified evidentiary material is found to be defective, restoration work needs to be done.

A digital data investigation technique known as *digital forensics* is essential to such data restoration. For example, if an email message that can be used as favorable evidence for a Japanese client company has been erased, how can it be restored? Can it be restored even if the email software program used is not a common one like Outlook and Gmail, but a program internally developed by the client company?

To address such problems, it is essential to select a provider with advanced digital forensic skills that can deal with uniquely Japanese problems. As Japanese-language data are recorded in a multibyte code, it is important to select a provider with suitable forensic skills if an in-depth investigation is to be conducted.

JAPANESE COMPANIES' PERCEPTION OF EDISCOVERY-RELATED PROBLEMS

In typical cases, even if a problem occurs, Japanese companies do not recognize its presence because they are not notified of its presence by their service providers until later. They are surprised and angered when they receive a bill inflated by the extra discovery-related work required to resolve the problem. When this type of scenario arises, some companies direct their anger toward their attorneys and take actions such as replacing the attorneys, demanding the submission of a more detailed statement of expenses, and asking for the reduction of legal fees.

For their part, the attorneys may regard such reactions as unreasonable and blame the clients for not making clear what they wanted in the first place. But in a case like this, Japanese client companies with little experience of eDiscovery cannot help feeling betrayed by their attorneys, as the eDiscovery service provider and attorney are one and the same in their eyes.

Of course, not all Japanese companies are uneducated about eDiscovery. An increasing number of companies are seriously considering how to better prepare for eDiscovery based on their own experiences. One example of the growing awareness about eDiscovery has been the adoption of eDiscovery tools by Japanese companies as part of their litigation strategy.

At one time, companies with a particularly high level of interest in litigation trends in the United States as well as trends in eDiscovery, adopted their own eDiscovery tools in an attempt to maintain proactive control over their own legal cases. The attempt reflected their awareness of the various risks that they might face if they lost such control. However, the introduction of discovery tools sourced from U.S. providers did not bring successful results. This was because although the tools introduced by the companies themselves were Japanese language-capable, the eDiscovery service providers selected by their attorneys in the event of litigation were not prepared to handle Japanese-language discovery. In one case that I know of, eDiscovery tools introduced by a Japanese company at a cost of more than $1 million dollars proved totally useless in litigation.

As described above, companies aware of the need to prepare for eDiscovery are taking actions. Corporate legal officers at Japanese companies who are involved with several legal cases in the U.S. are gradually accumulating experience and knowledge. Every month, UBIC holds seminars on strategic and preventive legal solutions for Japanese companies in partnership with U.S. law firms. Around 100 corporate legal officers attend these seminars, indicating Japanese companies' strong interest in these matters.

Corporate legal officers in Japan are generally working hard to become familiar with eDiscovery. As outside counsel, you would do well to remember that:

- You must support Japanese general counsel as litigation professionals.
- Your professionalism will be tested by your Japanese clients.
- You must understand that if you cling to the pretext that Japanese-language eDiscovery is problematic, that could be seen as a sign of ignorance on your part.

CHAPTER THREE

Identifying Ideal eDiscovery Service Providers for Japanese Companies

———————————————○———————————————

E arlier, I cited two key requirements for becoming a lawyer of choice for Japanese companies. One of these requirements was to understand how most Japanese companies think and, with that understanding in mind, communicate with the client through a manner and means that they would appreciate and find easy to understand. In this chapter, I will discuss the other requirement in more detail. It is key to determine the eDiscovery service provider's Japanese-language capability and take care to prevent Japanese client companies from suffering undue stress during the eDiscovery process.

Which aspects of potential eDiscovery service providers should you pay attention to in order to measure their Japanese-language capability and determine their suitability in order to avoid causing Japanese client companies undue stress during the eDiscovery process? There are four criteria that I believe matter most.

FOUR CRITERIA FOR MEASURING A PROVIDER'S CAPABILITY TO HANDLE JAPANESE-LANGUAGE EDISCOVERY

Criterion 1.
Experience Handling Discovery
Projects Related to Japanese Companies

First of all, it is important to ask in-depth questions about the provider's experience in handling eDiscovery projects related to Japanese companies. The body of knowledge accumulated through experience is the most important business asset for providers. Regarding discovery, the required skills and capabilities vary considerably from case to case. As sophisticated as the software programs the provider has may be, the eDiscovery process is likely to become inefficient if the discovery manager is not knowledgeable about Japanese-language discovery, forcing the client company and the attorney to perform extra work that would otherwise be unnecessary.

The following are examples of the right questions to ask.

- What kind of cases has the discovery service provider handled and for which companies?
- Does the provider have a discovery proposal tailored to meet the needs of Japanese client companies?

For provider salespeople with a bit of experience, talking about the theory of the eDiscovery processes as described in the Electronic Discovery Reference Model (EDRM) model, for example, would not be difficult. The important thing to look out for is whether the provider can explain specifically what they can do for your Japanese clients in practice.

You can judge the extent of the provider's experience with Japanese-language eDiscovery projects based on whether they can provide explanations about the specifics of actual processes of discovery work. Unfortunately, most local U.S. providers fail this test. As they focus mostly on subcontracting work, they only do what they are told to do by the prime contractors. As a result, such providers have little body of accumulated knowledge and may be incapable of proposing solutions of their own. The most you might expect from them is a vague promise like, "We will do our best for our customers." Some providers merely hand out promotional brochures explaining the software programs they use instead of providing more substantial information through a presentation or other means. It is nearly very likely that such providers will efficiently perform Japanese-language eDiscovery work.

As described above, the first criterion is whether the provider has experience in Japanese-language eDiscovery work and is aware of the unique aspects of such work.

Criterion 2.
Capability to Provide Services That Meet Japanese Companies' Needs

The second criterion is whether the eDiscovery service provider can offer services that meet the needs of Japanese client companies.

For example, in order to identify the characteristics of the services available from the service provider, you need to carefully examine the following points.

- The provider's understanding of Japanese corporate culture
- The personal characteristics and temperament of the provider's Discovery Manager
- Whether the provider's services are tailored specifically to Japanese-language discovery
- Whether the provider supports cloud service for data hosting
- Whether the provider can perform the whole of discovery work without transferring data out of Japan (or out of the company) if the client wishes
- Whether the provider can handle encoded Japanese-language files

Most service providers can probably offer fluent explanations about their discovery tools. However, it is important to ask them what knowledge and experience they have acquired in relation to the specific functions of their tools. The possession of practical knowledge, rather than technology and equipment, is the indicator of a provider's capability. Answers offered to questions about their experience in actual cases will reveal a given provider's characteristics and its area of strength. This second criterion will enable you to determine whether a provider's area of strength matches your client's needs.

Criterion 3.
Measuring the Service Provider's Competency Based on Whether It Asks the Right Questions

The third criterion is what kind of questions the eDiscovery service provider asks in relation to the discovery project. Typical questions that should be asked concern the client's IT system, including the types of IT systems and software programs, such as an internal document management system, file system, an email program, and an encoding program. It would be impossible to perform eDiscovery work without input on these matters, which are essential elements of the work.

If the provider has a prepared checklist concerning these essential points, that may be an indication of its systematic preparedness to perform eDiscovery work. However, if the service provider fails to ask questions about these electronic platforms, you should doubt its eDiscovery capability.

Another thing you may learn from the service provider's questions is its approach to the eDiscovery project. The provider may be merely trying to sell its software programs and systems, or it may be ready to provide the comprehensive discovery support you and your client are interested in receiving. The point is that you may find clues about the provider's competency by the questions it asks in relation to the eDiscovery project.

Criterion 4.
The Service Provider's Ability to Develop Japanese Language Discovery Support Tools (Systems)

The fourth and last criterion is whether the eDiscovery service provider can develop Japanese-language discovery support tools (systems) itself.

To some degree, eDiscovery support service providers must have the ability to customize software programs according to individual clients' needs. Therefore, it is most desirable to select a provider capable on its own of developing discovery support tools and systems. It is difficult for providers using tools licensed from other companies to meet the various needs of individual Japanese clients. Such providers cannot propose an alternative solution to clients facing problems arising from the use of tools not tailored to Japanese-language discovery work.

If providers do not have practical knowledge accumulated through the experience of providing discovery service using Japanese language-capable eDiscovery support tools (systems), they will not be able to provide the best possible solutions for clients. For example, eDiscovery providers whose main focus is on developing discovery support tools are not necessarily capable of appropriately managing Japanese-language eDiscovery projects. Even though they may be knowledgeable about the technical aspects of discovery support tools, such service providers tend to lack sufficient knowledge to provide practical advice about the use of tools. Moreover, even though they may be able to support clients as customer engineering support specialists, such providers may pay little attention to the litigation side of the discovery project.

Of course, the whole of eDiscovery work is supposed to be done under the supervision of the litigation attorney. All the same, information and knowledge necessary for improving the efficiency of eDiscovery work is mostly held by the discovery service provider. Preferably, the provider should have the capability to cooperate with the attorney in working out the best possible solution from the perspective of litigation, rather than merely doing what it is told to do as a subcontractor.

Most eDiscovery providers tend to underestimate the complexity of eDiscovery work. They see little need to customize tools according to their clients' needs or propose solutions themselves because, from their standpoint, discovery work is mostly finished when the archiving of documents is completed. Among Japanese companies as well, the view is widespread that eDiscovery work is little more than scouring computer files and extracting necessary documents. In reality, however, eDiscovery involves much more complex processes and necessitates in-depth knowledge.

Complex eDiscovery processes can best be appropriately performed if Japanese language-capable discovery tools developed by a Japanese service provider are used by the provider itself, which knows how best to use the tools effectively. The fourth criterion is the provider's ability to develop eDiscovery tools.

WHAT ARE THE DIFFERENCES BETWEEN SELF-PROFESSED "MULTILANGUAGE PROVIDERS" AND "ASIAN-LANGUAGE EDISCOVERY SPECIALISTS"?

The Asian-language eDiscovery specialist is, by my definition, a provider that meets all four criteria mentioned above.

What should be kept in mind is that from information available on company websites and promotional materials, which are full of terms like *multilanguage* and *multinational,* it is difficult to identify Asian-language (such as Japanese language) eDiscovery specialists from among all those providers that claim to be multilanguage providers.

What sets Japanese-language eDiscovery specialists apart from self-professed multilanguage providers?

Broadly speaking, there are differences in two aspects: technical support and communications capability. Let's assess these factors now.

Differences in Technical Support

To avoid going too far into technical details, let me focus on the following two points that indicate whether a service provider is a Japanese-language eDiscovery specialist. The first point is whether the provider is Japanese language-capable in all processes of eDiscovery. Every eDiscovery service provider has strengths and weaknesses. Some providers are superior in server hosting capability, while others focus on selling discovery tools. But most providers are not Japanese language-capable in all processes of eDiscovery.

For the moment, our company is probably one of very few providers in the world that are really Japanese language-capable in all processes of eDiscovery. Most of the self-professed multilanguage providers are Japanese language-capable only in the data collection process and lack sufficient capability to appropriately handle Japanese documents in other processes.

Although it may be obvious, I would like to emphasize yet again the importance of selecting a provider that is Japanese language-capable in all processes of eDiscovery.

The second point is whether the provider makes specific efforts to facilitate Japanese-language eDiscovery work, such as taking steps to prevent character garbling. Japanese-language eDiscovery specialists use the "pretreatment" technique to ensure accurate recognition of Japanese characters in the analysis process. Without pretreatment, character garbling may occur in Japanese texts, impeding keyword-based searches. The pretreatment, which makes it possible to complete eDiscovery without being constrained by the problem of character garbling, is a unique technique offered by only a few self-professed multilanguage providers.

Differences in Communications Capability

Asian-language eDiscovery specialists and self-professed multilanguage providers also differ in their communications capability. If you select an Asian-language eDiscovery specialist, your Asian clients will be able to communicate with the provider in their native language without feeling stress, just as U.S. clients smoothly communicate with U.S. providers in English.

Another advantage of Asian-language eDiscovery specialists is that they have critical facilities such as a data center and an eDiscovery research laboratory in each country, making it possible to perform the whole of eDiscovery work without transferring data out of clients' home countries. Because Asian-language eDiscovery specialists also have cross-border support systems, such as these, they can deploy support staff to either the United States or within Asia.

Superiority in technical support and communications capability are the most obvious examples of the advantages of hiring Asian-language eDiscovery specialists rather than self-professed multilanguage providers.

If a provider is to be called an Asian-language eDiscovery specialist, it must have superiority in these two points at the least.

HOW TO IDENTIFY IDEAL EDISCOVERY PROVIDERS FOR JAPANESE COMPANIES

To help lawyers recommend competent providers to Japanese client companies, I will explain in more detail how to identify ideal eDiscovery providers for Japanese-language discovery projects.

As you know, eDiscovery comprises several processes. It is important to identify providers that can provide the best possible solution in each process while taking into consideration the unique characteristics of Japanese companies. These processes, as described in the EDRM, are:

- Data identification.
- Data preservation.
- Data collection.
- Data processing.
- Data analysis.

- Review.
- Production of documents to be submitted.

Below, I will explain the checkpoints for identifying providers that can provide effective eDiscovery support to Japanese companies. Of course, the checkpoints will be useful for selecting providers for U.S. clients as well.

UNDERSTANDING THE UNIQUE CHARACTERISTICS OF JAPANESE COMPANIES AND ORGANIZING EFFECTIVE PRE-PRESERVATION MEETINGS ARE CRITICAL TO DATA IDENTIFICATION

Data identification, a catalog of the specific characteristics including character encoding and extraction of metadata, which is the first step of eDiscovery, is a particularly important process. As in the case of discovery projects in the United States, eDiscovery providers conduct a data-mapping process after identifying custodians and locating potentially relevant data. In some cases, IT system workers at the client company perform the data-mapping process under the instruction of the eDiscovery provider.

Understanding the unique characteristics of Japanese companies is important for data identification concerning documents held by the companies. You must select an eDiscovery service provider with an in-depth understanding of those characteristics. The provider needs to consult with the corporate legal officer of the client company about how to proceed with the project and how to handle internal communications while taking into account various factors, including the client's corporate culture, organizational structure, and relationship with the attorney as well as how well-informed about eDiscovery the officer is.

Identification as Preparation for Preservation

In preparing for the preservation of data, also understood as forensic collection and processing, it is essential to understand the status of data held by the client company by checking on the following points:

- What IT systems does the Japanese client company use?
- What is the company's security system like?
- What is the company's server status?
- What kind of data encoding program is the company using?

The data identification process provides the opportunity for a *pre-preservation meeting*. During this meeting, the provider not only receives information on the status of data, but discusses with the client various arrangements, including scheduling and the means of data extraction. In some cases, the provider may perform the preservation process after the client has collected data itself and uploaded them to its own server. In other cases, the provider may obtain necessary passwords from the client and copy all files stored in custodians' computer hard discs.

It is also essential to consider in advance what to do when files cannot be appropriately copied. At this stage, the service provider must brief the client on problems that may occur during discovery work, propose specific solutions (for example, when forensic copying is impossible because of a hard disc defect, file-level copying may be proposed as a reasonable alternative solution, based on the instructions of the litigation attorney), and decide which solutions should be provided when necessary.

How to extract relevant data from encoded files is a typical issue that comes up at this phase in eDiscovery. The service provider must make sure to check the encoding technique used by the client, as many Japanese companies use their own unique techniques.

In principle, electronic data should not be modified during discovery. However, encrypted data needs to be decrypted. eDiscovery providers should propose the best possible option so that the attorney can make the right decision. The treatment of encrypted data—whether the client itself will decrypt the data in advance or entrust the eDiscovery provider with the job—and other matters, including scheduling, should also be determined.

Another key issue is when data should be taken out of the IT system. If data are extracted from the server while employees are accessing the system, business operations may be disrupted. If custodians are away from the office on a business trip, for example, it is necessary to decide when the data in their possession should be extracted. A good Japanese eDiscovery service provider will be aware of necessary privacy and employment law issues related to collecting data.

About half a day is devoted to a pre-preservation meeting, as very careful preparation is necessary. Particularly, when the number of custodians reaches a certain number, for example 100 or more,

All these preparations involve delicate matters that must be handled by providers familiar with Japanese corporate cultures and business practices.

Agenda of a Pre-preservation Meeting

The agenda of a pre-preservation meeting is set by the eDiscovery service provider. If the provider is experienced in performing eDiscovery work for Japanese companies, it will be able to prepare the agenda best suited to the needs of Japanese companies. If the provider is experienced enough to make necessary arrangements without prodding from the attorney, then the attorney doesn't need to be particularly knowledgeable about Japanese-language discovery.

When the eDiscovery provider does not make necessary arrangements or participate in a pre-preservation meeting, you must keep a careful watch. Also, if the attorney tries to fully take charge of discovery-related preparation and arrangements with the client, a pre-preservation meeting will be held without the presence of the service provider and there will be no preliminary communications between the client and the provider. In that case, should a discovery-related issue occur, the lawyer will have to deal with it himself/herself and litigation procedures may be hampered.

If there is sufficient preliminary communication, most problems may be avoided or prepared for. Usually, problems are caused by a lack of communication.

Although there is a widespread perception among many Japanese companies that eDiscovery work disrupts their business operations, disruption can be avoided if proper procedures are followed.

JAPANESE-LANGUAGE DIGITAL FORENSIC CAPABILITY IS CRITICAL TO DATA COLLECTION

The key to the data collection process in Japanese-language eDiscovery projects is the eDiscovery provider's Japanese-language digital forensic capability. eDiscovery providers that do not possess this capability cannot deal with problems such as data copying failure.

Various other problems cannot be resolved without such capability, either. For example, potentially relevant data may be lost, damaged, deleted, or overwritten during litigation hold. Problems like these could occur particularly at Japanese companies that aren't experienced in discovery. To resolve them, eDiscovery providers need to have Japanese-language digital forensic capability, as some Japanese companies use email software programs and operating systems used only in Japan.

In some cases, it is necessary to verify the quality of digital data containing evidence. Typically, the chain of custody (COC) and evidence sheet are used to verify the quality of such data. The COC, which is a record of the custody and transfer of evidence, verifies the continuity of evidence custody. Meanwhile, an evidence sheet verifies that evidence contained in the submitted data has been preserved through such means as forensic copying of computer hard disc data, for example.

Naturally, the COC and evidence sheet may be required in Japanese-language eDiscovery projects as well. Electronic data containing evidence are usually submitted together with the COC and evidence sheet. When evidence is submitted, photographic records of evidence preservation are also attached in order to verify the reliability of the submitted materials when necessary.

PRETREATMENT OF DOCUMENTS IS CRITICAL TO DATA PROCESSING

In the data processing of Japanese-language eDiscovery, the pretreatment of capturing the proper character encoding and extraction of all useful metadata that I mentioned earlier is important. You must make sure to check whether the provider is conducting the pretreatment to make it possible to appropriately extract and analyze Japanese-language documents.

As I pointed out earlier, the effectiveness of keyword-based searches and the frequency of character garbling vary widely depending on whether the documents have undergone pretreatment.

KEYWORD IDENTIFICATION IS CRITICAL TO DATA ANALYSIS

In the analysis process, search functions including keyword-based search, concept-based search, linear search, and domain search are frequently used. The most important capability in the analysis process is keyword identification. In other words, the service provider must have sufficient experience to figure out which search queries should be used to comprehensively cover documents that the lawyer may need as evidence. This process requires a particularly high level of Japanese-language capability as well as an understanding of the IT system used by the client. Without Japanese-language capability, it is impossible to come up with the right set of search queries.

Different people use different search queries to obtain information on the same subject matter. The differences are even greater among people with different cultural and social backgrounds. In eDiscovery work for Japanese companies, keyword-based searches should be conducted by people familiar with Japanese culture and business practices based on their own business experience in Japan. In short, keyword identification is critical to eDiscovery work.

To achieve accurate search results, a wide variety of words and phrases are used in search queries. With regard to Japanese texts in particular, the presence of the *katakana* and *hiragana* syllabaries in addition to Chinese characters makes the keyword-based search all the more complex. Search efficiency varies widely depending on the search conditions set. The coexistence of the various character sets is a unique aspect of the Japanese language, and it is difficult even for native Japanese speakers to find relevant documents through the keyword-based search unless they have the necessary knowledge.

In keyword search, it is also essential to identify frequently used words and phrases that are similar to the keywords, and set the search conditions so as to exclude them from the search results. This step helps keep search results focused on those documents with the greatest potential to be responsive to the matter at hand. Providers of eDiscovery services, experienced in Japanese-language discovery, would be ready to propose solutions in this respect as well.

Keyword identification may be primarily a prerogative of lawyers. However, it is obvious that Japanese language-capable eDiscovery providers that are familiar with the Japanese business world are better positioned than many American lawyers to know which search queries to use to find Japanese documents related to an antitrust case concerning auto parts, for example. The keyword identification capability is a critical element of discovery work for Japanese companies.

JAPANESE LANGUAGE-CAPABLE REVIEW TOOLS AND MANAGEMENT ARE CRITICAL TO THE REVIEW PROCESS

In the review process concerning Japanese-language documents, it is imperative that Japanese language-capable review tools be used. Otherwise, document analysis would become a waste, however accurate it may be.

Problems in eDiscovery work for Japanese companies come to light in the review process. The consequences of problems such as unsuccessful data culling resulting from an inadequate Japanese-language analytical capability may somehow be dealt with in the review process if a sufficient amount of time and money is invested. However, if the review tool is not fully Japanese language-capable, it is impossible to appropriately review documents. If the review screen is full of garbled characters, there will be nothing to do other than to wait for the service provider to resolve the garbling.

It is also essential to select a provider that can manage the review process in a way suited specifically to Japanese-language documents. The key elements of review management are:

- Recruiting and educating reviewers.
- Monitoring reviewers.
- Creating a comfortable working environment.
- Performing the review process in Japan.

Recruitment and Education of Japanese Language-Capable Reviewers

The recruitment of Japanese language-capable reviewers is important. Although it is acceptable to use the same reviewers in several eDiscovery projects, the discovery manager must take care to avoid assigning an overload of work. The number of reviewers necessary per case varies from around a dozen to several hundred depending on the scale of the case. The largest case in which I was involved, employed around 300 reviewers.

Regarding eDiscovery work for Japanese companies, it is most desirable to employ reviewers who are native Japanese speakers. If you try to recruit a large number of Japanese language-capable reviewers in the United States, it may be difficult to ensure a consistent quality level among the review staff compared to what may be attainable in Japan.

Even though it is not necessarily difficult to recruit Japanese language-capable reviewers in the United States, employing 100 such reviewers (not to mention such a large number of native Japanese speakers) all at once would be no easy task. A job offer for Japanese language-capable reviewers in the Unites States may attract applications from people with various levels of language capability, including those of dubious capability, as the wages offered are typically higher than those offered to English-language reviewers. If the provider applies rigorous screening criteria, the quality of the review staff may be ensured. However, not all providers apply rigorous criteria, and as a result, people with inadequate Japanese-language skills may be included in the review staff, jeopardizing the accuracy and speed of the review work.

Recruiting reviewers in Japan and performing the review process there, rather than in the United States, is the best possible option for the review of documents held by Japanese companies. Doing so will reduce the risk of employing people with questionable Japanese-language capability and will also lower the personnel cost.

How should Japanese language-capable reviewers be trained? Reviewers should receive at least a whole day of training before starting the review work. Although there may be no problem with the Japanese-language capability of reviewers recruited in Japan, most of them, except for people who have the experience of living in the United States for an extended period of time or who have been involved in the litigation business, are not familiar with the discovery procedure. Unless they undergo sufficient training, they may not fully realize the gravity of the responsibility they take on as reviewers. As documents handled by reviewers often contain classified corporate information, it is important to have them understand their responsibilities through training, in addition to having them sign a pledge of confidentiality.

After the review starts, it is important to maintain close communication with reviewers through meetings. Meetings will provide the opportunity for reviewers to ask questions and for the eDiscovery service provider to brief them on specific procedures such as coding. Conducting such communications in Japanese will help to facilitate the review process of Japanese-language eDiscovery work.

Monitoring Reviewers

A numerical benchmark for the review speed—the minimum number of files to be reviewed per hour, for example—should be set, and reviewers' performance should be monitored as necessary based on the benchmark. In addition to the review speed, the quality also should be monitored based on a sampling of the documents that have been reviewed.

If a certain reviewer is conspicuously ahead of or behind others in the review progress, it is important to carefully examine the cause of the discrepancy. In addition to checking specifically how the reviewer is proceeding with his or her work, it may also be necessary to reexamine the reviewer's Japanese-language capability if he or she is a bilingual person.

Creating a Comfortable Working Environment

To ensure efficient and high-quality review, it is important to create a comfortable working environment for reviewers. Some eDiscovery providers, whether in Japan or in the United States, provide a poor working environment for reviewers. A stressful environment such as an overcrowded, windowless room would undermine the efficiency of the review work.

My company pays careful attention to the health management of reviewers, including stress management. We take care to keep the conditions of the review office comfortable through the use of humidifiers and air cleaners in wintertime, for example. Moreover, the discovery manager makes sure to have reviewers take time off as necessary.

Also important is motivation management. Appointing a skillful reviewer as a team leader helps to keep the review staff motivated throughout the review process.

Performing the Review Process in Japan

Most Japanese companies prefer to keep watch on the review process firsthand, so they will appreciate it if the whole of the review process is performed in Japan so that they can periodically visit the review office. Although from the standpoint of American lawyers it might be desirable to perform the review process in the United States, doing the review work in Japan also has merit. For example, as the client can see the review progress with its own eyes, the lawyer's reporting to the client will go smoothly. Periodic visits to the review office by the client may also help to keep a sense of discipline among the review staff.

To avoid raising suspicion that your law firm is trying to keep the client in the dark, make it possible for your clients to have easy access to the review process and to information on its progress.

Few eDiscovery service providers take the trouble to ensure careful management of the review process. Some providers do not care about efficiency, as slow progress could benefit them by enabling them to charge extra fees for increased review time. Such providers may take no action even if they find laggards among the review staff and may try to solve the problem by increasing the staff size. Providers with a high level of professionalism would not take such an irresponsible approach to their management of the review process.

As professionals in the eDiscovery field, providers are responsible for assembling a review team with a high level of Japanese-language capability. Merely assembling a team of reviewers with skills and knowledge is not sufficient to efficiently conduct coding work that meets the rigorous standard required in tough investigations in antitrust and other cases. The important thing for providers to do is to make proactive efforts to keep reviewers highly motivated and improve their performance.

THE FUTURE OF AUTOMATED REVIEW

Although I have discussed the management of the review process and review staff, the review process is likely to change rather dramatically in the future. In the discovery industry, automated review is attracting attention as a way of reducing the cost and time, including the cost of managing a human review staff.

Until now, human review has been an essential element of the process of reviewing documents to select evidence materials to be submitted to opposing parties and authorities. Lawyers and paralegals satisfy human review needs and in some cases more than 200 such professionals engage in an eDiscovery project for over two years. However, advances in technology have made it possible to streamline the review process through the use of technology-assisted automated review, also known as computer-assisted review.

Technology-assisted review, also known as TAR, which is based on artificial intelligence technology, and is used to reliably classify documents in an initial phase of the review process, although the litigation attorney is responsible for conducting final checks. To be specific, the TAR process assigns a relevance score to documents for the purpose of classification. Estimated accuracy can approach more than 90 percent. The use of TAR is growing in legal cases, which is creating a body of legal precedent in the use of the technology and its results.

TAR uses a process known as *predictive coding*, which enables an ultra-high-speed review, estimated in some cases to be 4,000 times faster than human review. In this case, adopting automated review is equivalent to assembling a team of 4,000 reviewers with advanced legal knowledge. A number of independent studies have concluded that TAR is superior to human review in accuracy as well as in efficiency.

The graph below shows an interesting finding concerning the accuracy of human review (in a study done by UBIC in New York in 2013).

1st and 2nd Days' Reviewer Score Distribution

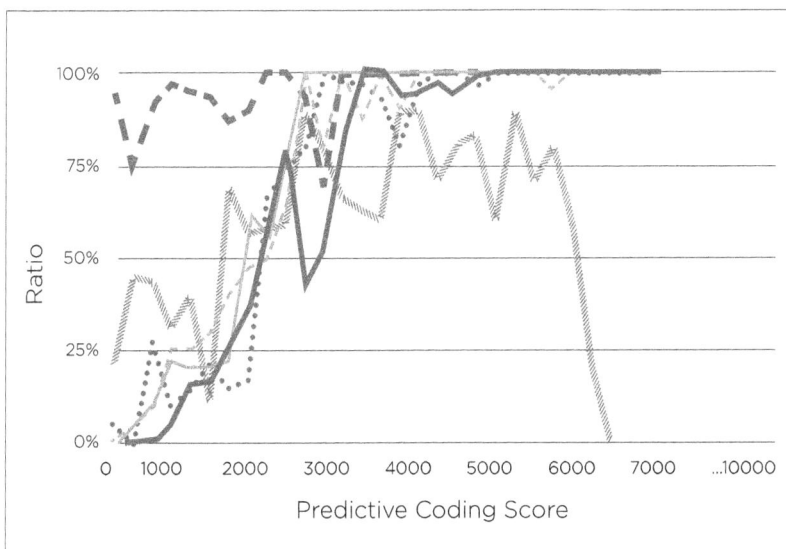

The graph shows the relevance scores assigned by the predictive coding-based automated review to the documents reviewed by five reviewers (Reviewers 1 to 5). The vertical axis represents the volume of documents judged to be relevant by the reviewers and the horizontal axis represents the relevance scores assigned by the automated review. On average, documents that received scores of 3,000 or less based on the automated review were judged to be irrelevant by the reviewers. However, Reviewer 1 and Reviewer 4 tended to judge documents with score points of 3,000 or less to be relevant while rejecting those with high scores as irrelevant.

As shown by this case, some reviewers cannot judge the relevance of documents accurately, although such inaccuracy in the first review phase may be resolved by final checks by the attorney. In the above-mentioned case, Reviewer 1 and Reviewer 4, who apparently failed to judge relevance accurately, were instructed to improve, but their performance did not improve and they were dismissed.

The point is that human review is inefficient given inevitable inconsistencies across a review staff in terms of speed and accuracy. Not only is TAR estimated to increase the review speed 4,000-fold but it can reduce review costs by more than half. A review project that would take more than two weeks to be completed by human review can be finished in a matter of hours by a well-monitored TAR program.

If one party in a legal case uses predictive coding for its review and the other party relies on human review, the latter would be put at a great disadvantage in terms of cost, time, accuracy, and labor.

Although TAR is not yet as popular as it is likely to become, it is certainly the trend of the future judging from recent developments in the U.S. litigation business. If the volume of documents handled by human reviewers can be minimized through the adoption of a technology like this, the day may come when the manual review process I mentioned earlier becomes a thing of the past.

COST MINIMIZATION, QUICK RESPONSE, AND MULTIFORMAT ADAPTABILITY ARE CRITICAL CHALLENGES FOR EDISCOVERY SERVICE PROVIDERS IN PRODUCTION OF RESPONSIVE DOCUMENTS

Let's now look at ways to solve three critical challenges in the production process in Japanese-language eDiscovery projects.

Minimizing Translation Costs

First, it is important to minimize translation costs. Translation is where there is the greatest opportunity for cost reduction in the Japanese-language eDiscovery process. In most cases, translation costs can be reduced by performing translation after other processes. In other words, all documents should be handled in the original language until relevant documents are identified, thereby ensuring that the volume of translated documents is kept to a minimum.

Quick Response

Second, quick response is essential. If an eDiscovery service provider is to take action quickly on the instruction of the client's lawyer, it needs to understand Japanese texts and be familiar with the file formats used by clients, which may include uniquely Japanese formats as well as the custody status of documents.

Attorneys may issue new instructions in rapid succession in the run-up to the deadline for the production of evidence. It is critical that the eDiscovery provider have the ability to respond immediately to the instructions to ensure that evidence is produced in time. Naturally, the service provider must take great care to prevent inadvertent submission of nonresponsive documents.

In discovery, the deadline for the production of evidence is sacrosanct. To make sure to meet the deadline, the provider must be prepared to work overtime and on holidays. It is a critical issue whether the eDiscovery provider has the willingness and flexibility to work around the clock and on a 365-day-a-year basis if necessary to meet the lawyer's demands.

Multiformat Adaptability

In the production process, the third critical challenge eDiscovery service providers must solve is multiformat adaptability. This issue also relates to quick response. The required formats vary from case to case. An eDiscovery provider prepared to handle several possible sets of formats that may be required will become your strong partner.

IS IT NECESSARY TO USE DIFFERENT PROVIDERS FOR ENGLISH AND JAPANESE-LANGUAGE EDISCOVERY PROJECTS?

I am frequently asked if it is necessary to change eDiscovery service providers according to the language involved. Selecting a suitable provider according to the language involved, whether English or Japanese, and managing the service provider appropriately is critically important. That will be an essential risk-management step in proceeding with litigation projects. Encouraging your clients to take this step is part of your responsibility as their attorney.

In the United States, there is a multitude of skillful eDiscovery providers, most of which are adept in English-language eDiscovery work. Therefore, I understand that in legal cases fought between U.S. companies, discovery-related problems are not so frequent. However, in eDiscovery projects for Japanese companies, unforeseen problems may arise. By doing your utmost to prevent eDiscovery-related problems, you will be able to provide valuable service to your clients and fulfill your duties to them.

If you recommend to a Japanese client company an eDiscovery service provider that is not Japanese language-capable because of your own convenience or because you have a good relationship with the provider, you could be accused of neglecting your duties as the attorney should a discovery-related problem occur.

In the increasingly competitive litigation industry, clients are becoming more and more demanding in terms of cost and quality. This trend is particularly prominent among Japanese companies. In these circumstances, you will be able to set yourself apart from competitors and present yourself as a lawyer of choice for Japanese companies if you join hands with an eDiscovery provider capable of proposing outstanding solutions, such as a predictive coding technique tailored to the Japanese language.

CHAPTER FOUR

Developing Good Relationships with Japanese Companies

⸺○⸺

In this chapter, I will discuss in detail a key requirement when working with Japanese companies: understanding how they think so that you may communicate with them through means that they will appreciate and find easy to understand. If you are to proceed smoothly with eDiscovery projects for Japanese companies, it is essential to understand the companies' characteristics and their methods of communicating.

COMMUNICATING WITH JAPANESE COMPANIES

While not all companies within a country are the same, there are some high-level consistencies we can anticipate, culturally speaking. To sum up, whereas Americans prefer open, frank communications using explicit language, Japanese people favor indirect, roundabout communications based on implicit understanding.

"Kuki wo yomu" (in English, "Read the atmosphere"), a popular phrase among Japanese youth, is emblematic of Japanese people's preference, regardless of their age or gender, for communication based on implicit understanding. This phrase means, "Guess what one should do from the mood of the situation or from the looks of other people, and act accordingly."

Moreover, Japanese people generally tend to have an overly strong inclination to avoid conflict. They use ambiguous language as a means of avoiding conflict, and regard it as a virtue to convey their thoughts to one another without explicitly saying yes or no.

The table below compares a few of the general characteristics of the Japanese and American styles of communication.

AMERICANS	JAPANESE
Prefer definitive, frank, direct, clear, simple, concise language.	Prefer implicit and complicated language as well as honorific expressions and roundabout expressions in business communications.
Saying yes or no clearly is a principle of communication.	Not saying yes or no explicitly is viewed as a means of avoiding conflict, and seen as a virtue.
Professionals must communicate in simple terms and in a concise manner. A roundabout way of speaking is regarded as offensive.	Making oneself understood by conveying one's thoughts in a round-about manner is seen as a mark of sophisticated communication skill.
The same sentence has the same meaning in any context. For example, *yes* always means "yes."	The same sentence may have different meanings depending on the context and situation. Communication depends largely on nonverbal means, such as physical gestures.

Let's take a closer look now at Japanese corporate culture, focusing on the institutional characteristics of Japanese companies and their approaches to discovery.

INSTITUTIONAL CHARACTERISTICS OF JAPANESE COMPANIES

Strong Inclination to Avoid Conflict

The underlying element of Japanese companies' institutional characteristics is a strong desire to avoid conflict. In Japan, resolving disputes through outright confrontation, such as by going to court, is considered undesirable. You should understand that the Japanese have a stronger aversion to lawsuits than might be expected among Americans, and consider them unpleasant and shameful activities that should be avoided.

In particular, the Japanese businesspeople that lawyers may communicate with in legal cases, such as employees in corporate legal offices and intellectual properties departments, are likely to have a strong inclination to keep things quiet and protect themselves against the risk of being held accountable for their decisions and actions. The tendency to put off decisions in order to avoid taking responsibility is especially strong among businesspeople at major Japanese companies.

You may be irritated by the indecision of Japanese businesspeople who have inclinations like these. However, this is the Japanese way of conducting business. In the Japanese business world, continuing to work for the same company for many years, represented by the concept of "lifetime employment," is still seen as a virtue and continues to be a customary practice. Many people believe that people who work for the same company throughout their business career deserve more respect than people who frequently switch jobs, even though changing jobs may be a way of enhancing business skills or pursuing a more successful career.

Avoidance of Explicit Expressions

Due to their inclination to avoid conflict, Japanese people often express themselves in a roundabout way, instead of using explicit language. Because of this, in the Japanese business world, the following phrases may be used as an alternative to saying no.

- "That is very difficult."
- "I will do my best to do that."
- "Let me think it over."
- "I cannot say anything definite."
- "I will consider the matter."
- "I can see your point."
- "I will call you again.

Japanese businesspeople use phrases like these as a way of saying no implicitly. They have no intention of confusing you by using roundabout expressions. This is simply their customary manner of speaking, which is intended to avoid unnecessary conflict with other people. It is part of the wisdom of life they have acquired in Japanese society over the course of their lifetime. It is part of the essential code of conduct in the Japanese business world.

In order to guide and assist their Japanese clients to the best of their ability, it is important for American lawyers to always read into what Japanese people may be thinking behind their words. Sometimes Japanese clients refrain from expressing opposition to their attorney's proposals because they have the sense that it would be disrespectful to do so, although such reticence does not necessarily benefit either the attorney or the client.

Japanese people also have a tendency to regard lawyers as people who should be looked up to and kept at a respectful distance, as they would teachers and senior executives, rather than as their partners in litigation. It is important for the attorney to narrow the distance with the client and ask specific questions in order to clarify vague points and avoid misunderstanding.

Lack of Awareness about the Need to Protect Classified Information in the eDiscovery Process

How to protect information and intellectual properties held by client companies is an important area in eDiscovery projects for Japanese companies. Documents containing evidence that may be used in court include classified information. If information that should not be disclosed, or need not be disclosed, becomes available to competitors during legal proceedings, it could jeopardize the client company's business ventures. However, few corporate legal officers in Japan are aware of such risk.

In the Japanese business world, with the exception of a few major companies, the concept of protecting intellectual property has not taken root. Precisely for this reason, if you educate Japanese client companies about the need to preempt the risk of unnecessarily or inadvertently passing vital information to third parties, your service as a legal professional will be highly appreciated.

Lack of Preparedness for Litigation

Finally, you should keep in mind that few corporate legal departments at Japanese companies are strategically prepared for litigation. Corporate legal departments in the United States are staffed by legal support professionals on a permanent basis, and the outside attorneys work with the general counsel and other in-house legal professionals to map out a litigation strategy. At Japanese companies, however, there is a strong tendency to leave legal affairs to the discretion of outside attorneys.

This tendency has both merits and detriments for the lawyers involved. While the client company's hands-off attitude may make it easy for the attorney to manage legal strategy, the attorney may feel that the company is doing nothing itself. Moreover, although some Japanese companies send corporate legal officers to law firms in the United States as part of their training, an arrangement like this rarely produces substantial results because both the trainees and the accepting law firm regard it as little more than a ceremonial ritual.

Japanese corporate legal officers generally do not have a strong motivation to acquire the knowledge and experience necessary for litigation. This is an important point to remember.

JAPANESE COMPANIES' PERCEPTION OF DISCOVERY

Unfamiliarity with and Fear of Litigation and Discovery

Japanese companies are not accustomed to litigation. Unlike in the United States, litigation is not a fact of life in the Japanese business world. Consequently, in the eyes of Japanese companies, litigation is something unknown and frightening, and naturally, most are unfamiliar with discovery as a legal procedure.

To my understanding, some American lawyers find it difficult to handle certain legal cases for Japanese companies because of their unfamiliarity with and fear of litigation in general and discovery in particular. Because they know little about discovery, they do not show willingness to cooperate in submitting documents and engaging in other discovery processes. To ameliorate this condition, know that when Japanese client companies appear to be uncooperative in an eDiscovery project it is likely an indication of their lack of understanding of discovery, rather than a disapproval of an attorney's strategy.

Legal procedures and discovery processes that are familiar to U.S. corporations are often foreign to many Japanese companies. A lawyer's instruction, "We require access to your chief executive's computer files for discovery work," may sound completely alien to people working at Japanese companies. As Japanese companies are unaccustomed to discovery, the attorney may have to educate company executives and employees about discovery in order to persuade them to cooperate. An example might be to inform the Japanese company's principals of the fact that their opponent is also going through the same process and will also disclose evidence to them.

Another thing to keep in mind is that some Japanese companies use uncommon software programs, applications, and IT systems. Therefore, in eDiscovery projects for Japanese companies, it may be necessary not only to ensure the Japanese-language capability of discovery staff and eDiscovery tools, and also to customize the tools necessary to deal with unique software programs and IT systems in use at Japanese companies.

Lack of Awareness about Who Performs Discovery

I will explain in a little more detail Japanese companies' lack of understanding about discovery.

When a Japanese company is a party to an international lawsuit that involves discovery, it is not unusual for employees working in relevant business divisions to be unaware that discovery is ongoing. Even though some employees may be aware of the ongoing discovery, few know that actual discovery processes are being performed by a specialized discovery service provider. There is a widespread misunderstanding among Japanese companies that discovery processes are performed by the attorney or support staff from the law firm. Some Asian companies whose American subsidiaries are involved in legal cases that require discovery assume that the discovery work is being done by the subsidiaries themselves.

Although such misunderstandings as these may are far less likely to occur in the United States, such is the lack of understanding about discovery among Japanese companies. Therefore, it is important to educate your Japanese clients about discovery procedures from the beginning.

JAPANESE COMPANIES' PERCEPTION OF AMERICAN LAWYERS

What is Japanese companies' perception of American lawyers, generally speaking? Often, unfortunately, American lawyers aren't viewed in the most favorable light. Corporate legal officers in Japan generally think of American lawyers as difficult people to deal with. As a result of this preconception, and owing to unique cultural communications protocols, typical Japanese companies hesitate to engage in frank dialogue with American lawyers at the beginning. To be perfectly honest, they would prefer not to deal with American lawyers at all, or would like to have Japanese lawyers act as intermediaries.

An attitude like this is not a mark of disrespectfulness or hostility toward American lawyers. Remember, Japanese companies may have irrational fears. Just as the Japanese business world appears to be mysterious to you, the American litigation industry can be frightening to them.

TIPS FOR CULTIVATING GOOD RELATIONSHIPS WITH JAPANESE COMPANIES

When you are employed by a Japanese company as an outside legal counsel, how should you conduct communications with their corporate legal officers? Here are some tips for facilitating communications.

Characteristics of Japanese-Style Business Meetings

It is essential to understand the unique characteristics of business meetings in Japan. People participating in a business meeting in Japan for the first time will be surprised by the difference in the atmosphere of the meeting from what they are used to. Generally speaking, business meetings in Western countries are conducted according to strict schedules and leave little room for prolonged discussions. A typical American meeting is finished in an hour or less, as the discussion is focused on the key points. A lengthy meeting full of prolonged discussions is likely to be viewed as unproductive.

Meanwhile, the definition of a successful meeting is very different in the Japanese business world because the decision-making process is different. At business meetings in Japan, importance is attached to forming a consensus through repeated discussions and based on feedback from various quarters. In the eyes of the Americans, Japanese-style meetings may seem inefficient. However, you should understand and respect this style of conduct as an important decision-making process in the Japanese business world.

The table below compares the characteristics of American-style and Japanese-style business meetings. Even though the characteristics described in the table are not always applicable, as an outsider to the culture it is important to be aware of how Japanese-style meetings are generally conducted so you may understand what kind of meeting is most comfortable for Japanese businesspeople.

AMERICAN-STYLE MEETINGS	JAPANESE-STYLE MEETINGS
Adopt a direct approach to issues.	Adopt an indirect approach to issues.
Aim to make things clear.	Aim to form a consensus.
Place emphasis on confirming facts.	Place more emphasis on coordinating interests than on confirming facts
Express opinions and provide explanations about confirmed facts.	Try to balance the interests of relevant parties.
Select the best option from the perspective of logic.	Avoid expressing opinions definitively.
The leader makes decisions.	Make decisions collectively.
Willingness to give and accept negative feedback is considered a mark of strength.	Take care to maintain dignity and pride by carefully choosing recipients of negative feedback and avoiding conflict as much as possible.
Use logic and persuasion when necessary to win an argument	Aim to build harmonious relationships that rely on communication based on implicit understanding.

Business Meeting Etiquette

American lawyers may be at a loss as to how to behave in business meetings in Japan. To explain the code of conduct, let's look at two forms of behavior that are likely to be viewed as a breach of etiquette.

Interrupting when someone else is speaking. At Western-style business meetings, it is not necessarily viewed as a breach of etiquette to interrupt when someone else is speaking, if the timing is right. However, Japanese business-people refrain from interrupting the speaker in principle. As the spirit of the maxim "Silence is golden" is upheld in Japanese society, it will be wise to wait until your turn to speak comes.

Speaking too fast. When you participate in a business meeting with a Japanese client, you may speak English with or without an interpreter. However, as most Japanese people are not accomplished English speakers, they may feel intimidated if you talk too fast. Therefore, you should take care to speak slowly. It will also be wise to ensure periodically that what you have said was accurately understood.

Next, I will give you examples of behavior frequently shown in Japanese business meetings that may bewilder or offend you, but which is mostly not regarded as inappropriate in the Japanese offices.

Responding to Bewildering Behavior

Although the five kinds of behavior cited below may seem inappropriate to Americans, I advise you to accept them philosophically as examples of cultural differences.

Whispered conversation during meetings. At Western-style meetings, engaging in whispered conversation while someone else is speaking is seen as a breach of etiquette. In principle, that should be true in Japan as well. All the same, whispered conversation during a meeting is not unusual in Japanese offices.

The sight of employees at a Japanese client company engaging in whispered conversation may lead American lawyers to suspect that the company may be institutionally secretive or that an individual has something to hide from them. However, such suspicions would be wrong. In a case like that, Japanese businesspeople are likely to be merely discussing some finer points of the agenda, rather than scheming. Although whispered conversation during meetings is generally frowned upon, the practice is nonetheless persistent in the Japanese business world.

Keeping eyes closed while listening to the speaker. During meetings, some Japanese people keep their eyes closed while listening to the speaker as a way of better concentrating on what is being said. Although this may appear bewildering to Americans, it is not an unusual practice in Japan. Remember that for some people, keeping the eyes closed while listening to the speaker is a way of strengthening mental concentration.

Responding to a question with a smile. As mentioned earlier, Japanese people have a strong inclination to avoid conflict. Some people therefore respond to yes-or-no questions with just a smile and without giving a clear answer. This attitude is likely to be an implicit way of saying no, or a sign of embarrassment. When people respond to a question with just a smile, they do not mean any ill, nor are they treating the question lightly. You should accept this kind of response as part of the Japanese way of communication. If you receive this kind of response from Japanese people, it is important to make efforts to encourage them to speak their minds.

Keeping silent. Silence is an important element of Japanese communication. In Western society, keeping silent during meetings is viewed as a sign of lack of interest or unwillingness to participate in discussions. However, when Japanese people keep silent, that is not necessarily an indication of lack of interest in the discussion. When people remain silent, they are likely either to be waiting for other people to ask for their opinion or to be thinking that silence suits that particular moment of the meeting. They uphold the spirit of the maxim "Speech is silver, silence is golden." Not making unnecessary or careless remarks is seen as a mark of high intelligence.

Indirect language. Japanese people feel uneasy expressing themselves in a direct way. They are likely to avoid direct language when voicing complaints like the following to an attorney.

- "Can't you reduce this excessive cost?"
- "Why can't you carry out the project according to schedule?"
- "You are slow in replying to our emails."

Although, ideally, the client should clearly express complaints like these at an earlier stage in discovery so that appropriate solutions can be found, individuals working in Japanese companies tend to refrain from saying something negative or unpleasant outright. You may as well accept this tendency as one of the institutional characteristics of Japanese companies.

All the same, you should not disregard what your Japanese clients may be thinking behind a wall of silence and vagueness. They are likely to be sending messages through indirect language.

Here are a few examples of indirect language that Japanese businesspeople may use to couch their complaints. When Japanese businesspeople say, "I was surprised because the cost was higher than I expected," what they really mean is, "Could you reduce the cost?"

When there is a delay in an eDiscovery project, you may receive an inquiry like this: "It seems that the project is not proceeding according to schedule. Am I correct in understanding that the delay cannot be helped?" Japanese businesspeople use a euphemism like this when what they really mean is, "Why can't you carry out the project according to schedule?" As voicing a complaint explicitly is considered unseemly in Japan, people tend to resort to euphemisms when conveying their dissatisfaction.

When you receive an email that says, "I understand that your schedule is busy, but I'm looking forward to an email reply from you," you should take that to mean, "Why can't you reply more quickly?" Japanese people use a roundabout way of speaking because they want to avoid conflict. In this case, the use of an indirect expression should not be mistaken for a lack of urgency for a quick reply.

If you fail to recognize the urgency or gravity of an issue amid the fog of roundabout and vague communication with a Japanese client and therefore sit on your hands without addressing the client's concerns, you may be surprised to be summoned abruptly by your boss after an angry phone call from the client. The important thing is to maintain close communication with the client while keeping in mind the need to read the meaning behind the words and accurately understand the client's needs, concerns, and requests.

How to Deal with Demands for Fee Reduction

I am often asked by American lawyers how to deal with Japanese clients' demands for fee reduction. Like their U.S. equivalents, Japanese companies try to keep a tight lid on legal expenses. How should American lawyers react when presented with a demand for fee reduction after submitting a cost estimate?

First of all, it is essential to consider where opportunities for possible cost cuts exist by reviewing the work processes in the discovery project. For example, translation costs may be reduced by delaying the translation process until after the identification of relevant documents. An eDiscovery service provider experienced in Japanese-language eDiscovery work may come up with ideas for cost reduction.

Second, it is important to explain the reason why your cost estimate is appropriate. Trying to achieve cost reduction by all means would not be wise. Even though service providers boasting of their low fees may offer a rock-bottom estimate, they may prove to be incapable of appropriately handling Japanese-language documents, making it necessary to employ another provider to do the work and pay extra fees. Selecting the right service provider on the basis of competency rather than cost will likely help keep costs low over the long run.

Before the start of the eDiscovery project, you should ask your service provider to prepare a cost simulation and to indicate what additional costs could arise in which process. As explained above, it is important to reduce the risk of additional expenses arising by selecting a competent provider. In most cases, Japanese client companies in eDiscovery projects are presented with an inflated bill because of cost overruns.

What might reduce costs? Eliminating character garbling, a feat you cannot expect low-cost providers to achieve, will reduce the cost of eDiscovery overall. Automated review that uses advanced review tools will also whittle down the cost of a project by drastically reducing the required number of human reviewers.

The important thing to do is to propose solutions for the client and review the cost estimates from the perspective of optimizing cost through quality improvement. This approach will help you to deal with demands from your Japanese client for fee reduction.

The Japanese Style of Wining and Dining: *Settai*

Settai is the Japanese style of wining and dining in which you may be included as a participant. In the Japanese business world, entertaining business clients, partners, and associates with food and drink is seen as a practice essential to the smooth conduct of business. Although this practice may appear alien to you, you may find it to be a useful way of developing good relationships and improving communication with the client.

Objective of settai. For Japanese companies, *settai* is an occasion for fostering mutual trust between host and guests in a relaxed atmosphere. Although it may not be unusual in the Western world to discuss business matters at dinner and drinking sessions, it is not common to talk about business matters or other formal topics in a Japanese *settai* session.

When you participate in a *settai* session hosted by a Japanese client company, it will be wise to let your host choose the topics of conversation. If your host brings up business matters, you may follow that lead. Otherwise, it is advisable to avoid talking about business matters.

Even if there is not any discussion of business matters during a *settai* session, the host is unlikely to view the occasion as a waste of time. Rather, a *settai* session is usually valued as an opportunity to look at clients, partners, and associates in a different light compared with interactions when engaging in business.

Social drinking. In Japan, social drinking is seen as an essential part of the relationship with business clients, partners, and associates, as well as coworkers. What is particularly notable about social drinking in Japan is that it is an opportunity for businesspeople to cast off the cloak of formality and communicate with one another in a relaxed atmosphere. In particular, social drinking is a means of deepening relationships through free-wheeling discussions.

In a *settai* session, failing to keep the glasses of the guests full all along is seen as a breach of etiquette on the part of the host. Your glass therefore will be refilled before you empty it. If you are not a strong drinker, it will be wise to drink slowly so that your glass remains at least half full. If someone offers to refill your glass, declining the offer with an apologetic smile would be the way out. If you explain that you are *geko* (a weak drinker), most Japanese would understand. Of course, responsible drinking is always advised.

IDEAL AMERICAN LAWYERS FOR HANDLING EDISCOVERY CASES FOR JAPANESE COMPANIES

To conclude this chapter, let us consider what the ideal lawyer, in the eyes of Japanese companies, is like. What kind of lawyer do they want to employ as their legal counsel?

Of course, the ideal legal counsel should have the ability to formulate a successful litigation strategy. However, I have the sense that it is more important from the perspective of Japanese companies that a lawyer understands Japanese corporate culture and the Japanese way of doing things and makes an effort to operate skillfully within the culture.

Lawyers who understand the Japanese corporate culture do not need to have overly high expectations for the level of their clients' globalization. Although globalization has become a popular concept in the Japanese business world, we should not assume that Japanese companies have necessarily adapted to globalization in the true sense of the word. I have the impression that Japanese companies are confusing globalization with internationalization. In their view, globalization is little more than expanding into foreign markets. However, globalization in the true sense of the word refers to the process in which various countries in the world become increasingly interconnected, rendering the national borders less relevant. It seems to be too early to expect all Japanese companies to embrace globalization.

American lawyers need not always conform to the Japanese way of conducting business. Lawyers must do their job from the perspective of efficiency, so I presume your sense of professionalism will prevent you from pandering to your clients' wishes when performing your job. You should not jeopardize the efficiency of your litigation projects or the quality of your legal service by kowtowing to clients.

The best thing to do to facilitate the attorney-client relationship in Japanese-language eDiscovery projects will be to employ an intermediary/coordinator who understands the circumstances and cultural backgrounds of both sides. Although some second-tier Japanese law firms act as such a coordinator, employing a lawyer with little knowledge of discovery as a go-between could undermine the attorney-client relationship.

Using an eDiscovery service provider like UBIC as a go-between will be worth considering as a realistic option. At first, you may feel uneasy about leaving it to an eDiscovery provider to handle communications with your client. However, if the provider manages the whole of communications related to eDiscovery, you can be assured of smoothly obtaining information necessary for litigation strategy and concentrate on strategy planning. This could speed the process, spare you and the client frustration, and help ensure excellent results.

CHAPTER FIVE

The Importance of Selecting an Asian-Language eDiscovery Specialist

———○———

In the previous chapters, I've explained the key points concerning the selection of eDiscovery service providers for Japanese-language discovery projects. You may be wondering specifically which eDiscovery provider you should select. I can assure you that UBIC, of which I am the chief executive officer, is able to provide your Japanese client companies the most efficient eDiscovery support services. UBIC is an Asian-language eDiscovery specialist and we are world leaders in eDiscovery support for Japanese and other Asian companies.

ESSENTIAL ATTRIBUTES OF AN ASIAN-LANGUAGE EDISCOVERY SPECIALIST

An Asian-language eDiscovery specialist must possess superior technical competency, support capability, and experience in handling Japanese-language eDiscovery projects.

Technical Competency

Most importantly, an Asian-language eDiscovery specialist must be capable of analyzing texts written in Asian languages, including Japanese. An Asian-language eDiscovery specialist has various means to provide solutions to problems specific to Asian languages (for example, multibyte character languages). Therefore, it can prevent character garbling, thereby achieving efficiency and accuracy at the same time in eDiscovery. By eliminating the need for superfluous work (for example, translation of documents before processing), an Asian-language eDiscovery specialist can optimize the cost and reduce the risk of scheduling delays.

One prominent emergent trend in eDiscovery is predictive coding, which applies artificial intelligence technology to the review process. UBIC is one of only a few companies in the world that have succeeded in developing a predictive coding technique tailored to the review of Asian-language documents. This technology is bringing about a revolution of sorts to the review process, which has been the most costly and time-consuming aspect of eDiscovery work.

The most advanced version of predictive coding emulates the document selection process of human reviewers. Results of document selection made by lawyers as a sample are used as teaching data for predictive coding. Only a relatively small percentage of all documents to be reviewed are handled by human reviewers, with the rest being taken care of by automated review using predictive coding. Based on the teaching data, relevance scores are assigned through our own algorithm to keywords specific to the discovery project, thereby making it possible to automatically identify potentially relevant documents. In essence, using the automated review is equivalent to employing a team of dozens of professional lawyers for the review. Predictive coding has made such progress in the level of accuracy it achieves that its review results are shown to be more accurate on average than the results of human review.

At UBIC, we've realized the practical use of advanced predictive coding ahead of other eDiscovery service providers. Our advanced predictive coding technique drastically reduces the time spent on the most time-consuming aspect of the review process (reviewing documents and extracting potentially relevant materials) and it achieves some of the highest levels of accuracy in the industry. In other words, our service enables early identification of relevant documents, which provides lawyers and their clients more time to plan their litigation strategy.

By adopting additional functions that improve review quality, advanced predictive coding has further raised the accuracy of review results while drastically reducing review time. Moreover, these additional functions, which include applications related to litigation hold and large-scale data analytics, also know as Big Data, have increased user convenience and better serve the needs of lawyers and their client companies. In order to review a vast amount of documents with a high degree of accuracy, it is increasingly important to take advantage of cutting-edge techniques such as UBIC's advanced predictive coding.

U.S. judicial authorities, including the courts and the Department of Justice, have recognized the validity of evidence materials extracted through predictive coding. If predictive coding is introduced in the review process, the cost of translating documents and employing reviewers may be halved. Another revolutionary change we anticipate is that the cost difference between Japanese-language and English-language eDiscovery projects will be minimized. In that sense, advanced predictive coding will also help to promote the principle of fairness that is enshrined in the American legal system.

Support Capability

In addition to the capability to develop and use tools and systems, practical knowledge is essential. Specifically, an Asian-language eDiscovery specialist must be capable of providing support related to uncommon software programs and applications used by Asian companies, and the service provider must have permanent support staff who are native speakers of the required Asian languages.

If you are to implement an Asian-language eDiscovery project smoothly, it will be much more efficient for you to leave it to an eDiscovery provider to handle procedures, such as transfer of data files, and check on such details as the software programs and applications used by the client than to do such work yourself. Using an eDiscovery provider whose staff can communicate in the client's native language will greatly help to alleviate the stress the client may feel.

Some eDiscovery providers have a total product support team that looks at eDiscovery projects from the perspective of litigation strategy. Team members with in-depth knowledge of both discovery processes and support tools work with project managers and process engineers to provide effective solutions. A professional support team like this will ensure smooth implementation of eDiscovery work.

Experience in Handling Japanese Language eDiscovery Projects

Providers of eDiscovery that do not have sufficient experience in handling Japanese-language eDiscovery projects cannot perform eDiscovery work appropriately no matter how competent they may be in the technical aspect and however broad the scope of their services is.

Abundant experience in handling Japanese-language eDiscovery projects related not only to civil cases, but also to antitrust and other cases, is key to effectively managing the whole aspect of eDiscovery work for Japanese clients.

Effective management includes the efficiency, accuracy, and cost of the work as well as communications with the client, thereby ensuring the quality of the entire eDiscovery project.

WHY UBIC CAN PROVIDE SOLUTIONS FOR JAPANESE LANGUAGE EDISCOVERY

UBIC has honed its technical expertise based on experiences acquired and lessons learned through its own business activities. Since we embarked on the eDiscovery support business in 2004, we have overcome a number of challenges. Upon founding the company, the first thing we did was to procure eDiscovery tools from American suppliers. When we used these tools to provide eDiscovery support for Japanese client companies, we were surprised to find them not useful in many respects. Even though we managed to preserve and collect documents, we were unable to accurately identify and extract potentially relevant documents. As a result, a vastly larger volume of documents had to be translated than would have been otherwise necessary, increasing the cost and time of the eDiscovery work and reducing the accuracy of the document review.

To resolve these problems, we launched a project to develop Asian language-capable eDiscovery support tools on our own. Since the development our first prototype support tool, we have upgraded our tools repeatedly. We now issue an upgrade every quarter.

Creating an environment that enables efficient technological development is critical to consistently producing upgraded versions at such a high frequency. Thanks to the use of an automated testing system, we can finish the process of identifying bugs of new products in just a day. In addition, because field system operators and developing engineers share offices, they can maintain close communication with each other and easily work together to identify bugs.

I believe that underlying Japan's technological prowess are traditional Japanese virtues, such as meticulousness, sensitivity, and conscientiousness. Japan excels in embodying the spirit of "God is in the details," a maxim upheld in some industries like construction and IT system development. My own experiences have convinced me that excellence in manufacturing and the spirit of "Customers first" that are hallmarks of Japanese industry are critical factors in the field of eDiscovery as well.

UBIC's Role as an Asian eDiscovery Support Provider: NASDAQ IPO

In May 2013, UBIC went public on the U.S. NASDAQ market. The path to the initial public offering was strewn with challenges. In Japan, we faced skepticism about our IPO plan from various quarters. Some people questioned the ability of a Japanese venture company like UBIC to successfully conduct an IPO in the United States, while others suggested that an IPO on the Tokyo Stock Exchange would be a better option for raising funds. All the same, we went ahead with the NASDAQ IPO for the following reason. Going public on the U.S. NASDAQ market is a means to accomplish our mission as an Asian discovery support provider.

Around the world, the American legal system is viewed as being fair. However, the principle of fairness has not necessarily been maintained in the field of discovery. So far, a number of Japanese companies have been put at a disadvantage in discovery cases as a result of extra time and cost made necessary by documents written and stored in Japanese. As the Asian-language capability of most eDiscovery support providers is inadequate, problems such as frequent character garbling, resulting in unnecessary and duplicative processes, such as translating all files before data culling.

Our mission is to apply our technical expertise and superior support capability to level the playing field by eliminating the disadvantage Japanese companies endure compared to their Western counterparts. By achieving growth as an Asian eDiscovery provider, we will help to promote the maturity of the eDiscovery market and maintain the fairness of the American legal system. Our NASDAQ IPO is a significant step toward accomplishing this mission.

The important thing to remember is that the fast-growing eDiscovery industry is at an inflection point. Technological innovation is spurring changes in long-established standards of the industry from one moment to the next. UBIC itself is driving this change by contributing to the development of the eDiscovery market in Japan and the United States through our world-class technology. Our technological superiority as an eDiscovery service provider is unrivaled in Japan and in the United States. In particular, regarding Lit i View™, an electronic evidence disclosure support system we developed, we are releasing upgrades to the predictive coding function every quarter. In this field, we are a market leader in both Japan and the United States.

If UBIC, with its world-class technology, spearheads the establishment of the eDiscovery industry's global standards together with American service providers, it will bring benefits to American lawyers and their client companies in the United States and throughout Asia. There is no doubt that if you are to win Asian companies as clients, it is important for you to educate them about eDiscovery and recommend the right eDiscovery provider.

In the eDiscovery industry, we continue to witness unfortunate situations in which the security of clients' data is put at risk because of the failure of eDiscovery service providers or their acquisition by other companies, which is a result of the consolidation among service providers in this industry. We have addressed concerns over such risk by making our financial position clear for everyone to see by virtue of our listings on the Tokyo Stock Exchange and the NASDAQ Stock Market, each a major global capital market participant.

We are determined to continue to enhance our technical competency and service quality to continue to effectively support American lawyers overseeing eDiscovery projects for Japanese client companies. I am looking forward to working with you one day soon to aid Japanese companies in their litigation efforts.

About the Author

○

Masahiro Morimoto is CEO and Chairman of the Board of UBIC, Inc. He is one of the few Japanese entrepreneurs whose company's stock is listed on the Tokyo Stock Exchange (Mother's Index, 2007) and the NASDAQ Stock Market (Global Market, 2013; Global Select Market, 2014).

Founded in 2003, UBIC provides high-technology solutions that assist clients in handling cross-border litigation. It is the only company listed in the business segment of litigation assisting services. The company successfully launched the world's first eDiscovery assistance tools supporting the Chinese, Japanese, and Korean languages, which is accomplished by incorporating predictive coding technology developed based on research in the field of artificial intelligence. These eDiscovery assisting tools are being used in the most high-profile cross-border litigations in the world.

Morimoto graduated from the National Defense Academy of Japan and served on an escort ship of the Japan Maritime Self-Defense Force. He is a certified fraud examiner, a board member of the Institute of Digital Forensics, and a member of the Association for the Study of Security Science. He has published several books on discovery procedures and forensics, and has contributed articles on law enforcement and corporate risk management to different publications.

Masahiro Morimoto was born in Osaka and currently resides in Tokyo.

www.ingramcontent.com/pod-product-compliance
Lightning Source LLC
Chambersburg PA
CBHW060617210326
41520CB00010B/1369